www.kathyhutto.wordpress.com

kathyahutto@gmail.com

Love deeply.

Live fully.

Seek wholly.

Dear friends,

I have told my children that there are two things that I hope they learn from me above all else. Those two imperative things are to read the Bible and pray daily. I heard it once said that the Israelites could not eat stale manna. We, too, cannot rely upon past experiences in the Word. The Bible is alive and we need to read it every day because it is one of the tools God uses to speak to us. John Piper writes, if we believe "God reveals Himself primarily through...the Bible, [we] should long be the most able readers." A missionary friend ministering in a troubled area of the world shared with me that a refugee she is ministering to fled after being beaten for converting to Christianity. She escaped with a tiny little book in her language and was completely enthralled when she received an entire Bible. She sat for hours reading it. Most of us have ready-access to multiple copies of the Bible and, yet, often don't take seriously how precious and necessary the Word of God is.

For the word of God is living and active and sharper than any two-edged sword, and piercing as far as the division of soul and spirit, of both joints and marrow, and able to judge the thoughts and intentions of the heart. Hebrews 4:12, NASB

I've heard the Biblical version of the Christmas story probably every single year I've been alive and yet reading it again this year, God spoke to me in a fresh way. For example, the word, "haste," just stood out to me. The shepherds hurried to tell others about Jesus, and I was convicted about how often I don't even snail crawl to spread the good news. Do you see how His Word is truly active and fresh with new things each time we read it.

There's Just No Substitute for the Bible and Prayer. Period.

I love devotions and read one most mornings, but there's just no substitute for God's Word. I want to encourage you to begin making time In His Presence a priority.

I recently heard Beth Moore speak about her journal. She said she took one she'd been given and modified it to make it her own. She said it's relatively blank at the onset of the new year. She lifts it up to the Lord and prays that the Lord fill it and her year however He wills. Then, at year end, she closes it and thanks God for His work within those pages and her life.

What you are holding in your hands is my journal. It's what I have used for my own study and prayer time over the last few years. I hope it will be a blessing to you. It is my sincerest prayer that it will encourage you to spend time In His Presence—fall in love with Jesus, break free, and live victoriously!

For His glory,

Kathy Hutto

I Am...

Return here daily and read these truths to yourself at the start of each day.

I Am...

Loved.

The Lord your God is in your midst, a mighty One who will save; He will rejoice over you with gladness; He will quiet you by His love; He will exult over you with loud singing. Zephaniah 3:17, ESV

But now thus says the Lord, He who created you... "Fear not, for I have redeemed you; I have called you by name, you are Mine." Isaiah 43:1, ESV

Worthy.

You have been bought and paid for by Christ, so you belong to Him—be free now from all these earthly prides and fears. 1 Corinthians 7:23, TLB

Understood.

For we do not have a high priest who is unable to sympathize with our weaknesses, but one who in every respect has been tempted as we are, yet without sin. Hebrews 4:15, ESV

Helped.

God is our refuge and strength, a very present help in trouble. Psalm 46:1, ESV

Known.

O Lord, You have searched me and known me! You know when I sit down and when I rise up; You discern my thoughts from afar. You search out my path and my lying down and are acquainted with all my ways. Even before a word is on my tongue, behold, O Lord, You know it altogether. Psalm 139:1-4, ESV

Not Alone.

Fear not, for I am with you; be not dismayed, for I am your God; I will strengthen you, I will help you, I will uphold you with my righteous right hand. Isaiah 41:10, ESV

Verses I will Memorize (2 per month)

January

February

March

April

May

June

July

August

September

October

November

December

Family & Friends Birthdays and Anniversaries

January

_____

_____

_____

February

_____

_____

_____

March

_____

_____

_____

April

_____

_____

_____

May

_____

_____

_____

June

_____

_____

_____

July

_____

_____

_____

August

_____

_____

_____

September

_____

_____

_____

October

_____

_____

_____

November

_____

_____

_____

December

_____

_____

_____

I thank my God in all my remembrance of you, Philippians 1:3 ESV

Journaling Pages

Weekly ~

Prayer Journal Page

&

Daily ~

M-F, Bible Reading Journal Pages

Bible Reading

Today's Date _____

Scripture God led me to read today...

_____

_____

Journaling Notes...

_____

_____

_____

_____

_____

_____

_____

_____

_____

_____

_____

_____

_____

_____

_____

_____

_____

_____

_____

_____

_____

_____

_____

_____

_____

_____

_____

_____

_____

_____

Bible Reading

Today's Date _____

Scripture God led me to read today...

_____

_____

Journaling Notes...

_____

_____

_____

_____

_____

_____

_____

_____

_____

_____

_____

_____

_____

_____

_____

_____

_____

_____

_____

_____

_____

_____

_____

_____

_____

_____

Scripture God led me to read today...

Bible Reading

Today's Date _____

Scripture God led me to read today...

_____

_____

Journaling Notes...

_____

_____

_____

_____

_____

_____

_____

_____

_____

_____

_____

_____

_____

_____

_____

_____

_____

_____

_____

_____

_____

_____

_____

_____

_____

_____

_____

_____

Bible Reading

Today's Date _____

Scripture God led me to read today...

_____

_____

Journaling Notes...

_____

_____

_____

_____

_____

_____

_____

_____

_____

_____

_____

_____

_____

_____

_____

_____

_____

_____

_____

_____

_____

_____

_____

_____

_____

_____

_____

_____

Prayer

Week of _____

Praise: Father, great are Your works! They are pondered by all who delight in them. Glorious and majestic are Your deeds, and Your righteousness endures forever. You have caused Your wonders to be remembered; You, Lord, are gracious and compassionate. (Psalm 111:2-4) The works of Your hands are faithful and just; all Your precepts are trustworthy. They are steadfast for ever and ever, done in faithfulness and uprightness. (Psalm 111:7-8)

Prayer List

Family — flip to the back section for strategic prayers

Name	Specific Prayer Need

Friends and Others (situations that I am made aware of)

Name	Specific Prayer Need

Answers to Prayers & Praises

Bible Reading

Today's Date _____

Scripture God led me to read today...

_____

_____

Journaling Notes...

_____

_____

_____

_____

_____

_____

_____

_____

_____

_____

_____

_____

_____

_____

_____

_____

_____

_____

_____

_____

_____

_____

_____

_____

_____

_____

Bible Reading

Today's Date _____

Scripture God led me to read today...

_____

_____

Journaling Notes...

_____
_____
_____
_____
_____
_____
_____
_____
_____
_____
_____
_____
_____
_____
_____
_____
_____
_____
_____
_____
_____
_____
_____
_____
_____
_____
_____
_____

Bible Reading

Today's Date _____

Scripture God led me to read today...

_____

_____

Journaling Notes...

_____

_____

_____

_____

_____

_____

_____

_____

_____

_____

_____

_____

_____

_____

_____

_____

_____

_____

_____

_____

_____

_____

_____

_____

_____

_____

Bible Reading

Today's Date _____

Scripture God led me to read today...

_____

_____

Journaling Notes...

_____

_____

_____

_____

_____

_____

_____

_____

_____

_____

_____

_____

_____

_____

_____

_____

_____

_____

_____

_____

_____

_____

_____

_____

_____

Bible Reading

Today's Date _____

Scripture God led me to read today...

_____

_____

Journaling Notes...

_____

_____

_____

_____

_____

_____

_____

_____

_____

_____

_____

_____

_____

_____

_____

_____

_____

_____

_____

_____

_____

_____

_____

_____

_____

_____

_____

_____

_____

Prayer

Week of _____

Praise: Father, great are Your works! They are pondered by all who delight in them. Glorious and majestic are Your deeds, and Your righteousness endures forever. You have caused Your wonders to be remembered; You, Lord, are gracious and compassionate. (Psalm 111:2-4) The works of Your hands are faithful and just; all Your precepts are trustworthy. They are steadfast for ever and ever, done in faithfulness and uprightness. (Psalm 111:7-8)

Prayer List

Family — flip to the back section for strategic prayers

Name   Specific Prayer Need

_____ - _____

_____ - _____

_____ - _____

_____ - _____

_____ - _____

_____ - _____

Friends and Others (situations that I am made aware of)

Name   Specific Prayer Need

_____ - _____

_____ - _____

_____ - _____

_____ - _____

_____ - _____

Answers to Prayers & Praises

_____

_____

_____

_____

Bible Reading

Today's Date _____

Scripture God led me to read today...

_____

_____

Journaling Notes...

_____

_____

_____

_____

_____

_____

_____

_____

_____

_____

_____

_____

_____

_____

_____

_____

_____

_____

_____

_____

_____

_____

_____

_____

_____

_____

_____

_____

Scripture God led me to read today...

Bible Reading

Today's Date _____

Scripture God led me to read today...

_____

_____

Journaling Notes...

_____

_____

_____

_____

_____

_____

_____

_____

_____

_____

_____

_____

_____

_____

_____

_____

_____

_____

_____

_____

_____

_____

_____

_____

_____

_____

Bible Reading

Today's Date _____

Scripture God led me to read today...

_____

_____

Journaling Notes...

_____

_____

_____

_____

_____

_____

_____

_____

_____

_____

_____

_____

_____

_____

_____

_____

_____

_____

_____

_____

_____

_____

_____

_____

_____

Bible Reading

Today's Date _____

Scripture God led me to read today...

_____

_____

Journaling Notes...

_____

_____

_____

_____

_____

_____

_____

_____

_____

_____

_____

_____

_____

_____

_____

_____

_____

_____

_____

_____

_____

_____

_____

_____

_____

_____

_____

_____

Bible Reading

Today's Date _____

Scripture God led me to read today...

_____

_____

Journaling Notes...

_____

_____

_____

_____

_____

_____

_____

_____

_____

_____

_____

_____

_____

_____

_____

_____

_____

_____

_____

_____

_____

_____

_____

_____

_____

_____

_____

_____

_____

Prayer

Praise: Father, great are Your works! They are pondered by all who delight in them. Glorious and majestic are Your deeds, and Your righteousness endures forever. You have caused Your wonders to be remembered; You, Lord, are gracious and compassionate. (Psalm 111:2-4) The works of Your hands are faithful and just; all Your precepts are trustworthy. They are steadfast for ever and ever, done in faithfulness and uprightness. (Psalm 111:7-8)

Prayer List

Family — flip to the back section for strategic prayers

Name   Specific Prayer Need

_____ - _____

_____ - _____

_____ - _____

_____ - _____

_____ - _____

_____ - _____

Friends and Others (situations that I am made aware of)

Name   Specific Prayer Need

_____ - _____

_____ - _____

_____ - _____

_____ - _____

_____ - _____

Answers to Prayers & Praises

_____

_____

_____

_____

Bible Reading

Today's Date _____

Scripture God led me to read today...

_____

_____

Journaling Notes...

_____

_____

_____

_____

_____

_____

_____

_____

_____

_____

_____

_____

_____

_____

_____

_____

_____

_____

_____

_____

_____

_____

_____

_____

_____

_____

_____

Bible Reading

Today's Date _____

Scripture God led me to read today...

_____

_____

Journaling Notes...

_____

_____

_____

_____

_____

_____

_____

_____

_____

_____

_____

_____

_____

_____

_____

_____

_____

_____

_____

_____

_____

_____

_____

_____

_____

_____

_____

Bible Reading   *Today's Date* _____

Scripture God led me to read today...

_____

_____

Journaling Notes...

_____

_____

_____

_____

_____

_____

_____

_____

_____

_____

_____

_____

_____

_____

_____

_____

_____

_____

_____

_____

_____

_____

_____

_____

Bible Reading

Today's Date _____

Scripture God led me to read today...

_____

_____

Journaling Notes...

_____

_____

_____

_____

_____

_____

_____

_____

_____

_____

_____

_____

_____

_____

_____

_____

_____

_____

_____

_____

_____

_____

_____

_____

_____

_____

Bible Reading

Today's Date _____

Scripture God led me to read today...

_____

_____

Journaling Notes...

_____

_____

_____

_____

_____

_____

_____

_____

_____

_____

_____

_____

_____

_____

_____

_____

_____

_____

_____

_____

_____

_____

_____

_____

_____

_____

_____

Scripture God led me to read today...

Prayer

Praise: Father, great are Your works! They are pondered by all who delight in them. Glorious and majestic are Your deeds, and Your righteousness endures forever. You have caused Your wonders to be remembered; You, Lord, are gracious and compassionate. (Psalm 111:2-4) The works of Your hands are faithful and just; all Your precepts are trustworthy. They are steadfast for ever and ever, done in faithfulness and uprightness. (Psalm 111:7-8)

Prayer List

Family — flip to the back section for strategic prayers

Name	Specific Prayer Need
_____ -	_____
_____ -	_____
_____ -	_____
_____ -	_____
_____ -	_____
_____ -	_____

Friends and Others (situations that I am made aware of)

Name	Specific Prayer Need
_____ -	_____
_____ -	_____
_____ -	_____
_____ -	_____
_____ -	_____

Answers to Prayers & Praises

_____

_____

_____

_____

Bible Reading

Today's Date _____

Scripture God led me to read today...

_____

_____

Journaling Notes...

_____

_____

_____

_____

_____

_____

_____

_____

_____

_____

_____

_____

_____

_____

_____

_____

_____

_____

_____

_____

_____

_____

_____

_____

_____

_____

_____

_____

Bible Reading

Today's Date _____

Scripture God led me to read today...

_____

_____

Journaling Notes...

_____

_____

_____

_____

_____

_____

_____

_____

_____

_____

_____

_____

_____

_____

_____

_____

_____

_____

_____

_____

_____

_____

_____

_____

_____

_____

Bible Reading

Today's Date _____

Scripture God led me to read today...

_____

_____

Journaling Notes...

_____

_____

_____

_____

_____

_____

_____

_____

_____

_____

_____

_____

_____

_____

_____

_____

_____

_____

_____

_____

_____

_____

_____

_____

_____

_____

_____

Bible Reading

Today's Date _____

Scripture God led me to read today...

_____

_____

Journaling Notes...

_____

_____

_____

_____

_____

_____

_____

_____

_____

_____

_____

_____

_____

_____

_____

_____

_____

_____

_____

_____

_____

_____

_____

_____

_____

Bible Reading   *Today's Date* _____

   Scripture God led me to read today...

_____

_____

   Journaling Notes...

_____

_____

_____

_____

_____

_____

_____

_____

_____

_____

_____

_____

_____

_____

_____

_____

_____

_____

_____

_____

_____

_____

_____

_____

   Scripture God led me to read today...

Prayer

Week of _____

Praise: Father, great are Your works! They are pondered by all who delight in them. Glorious and majestic are Your deeds, and Your righteousness endures forever. You have caused Your wonders to be remembered; You, Lord, are gracious and compassionate. (Psalm 111:2-4) The works of Your hands are faithful and just; all Your precepts are trustworthy. They are steadfast for ever and ever, done in faithfulness and uprightness. (Psalm 111:7-8)

Prayer List

Family — flip to the back section for strategic prayers

Name   Specific Prayer Need

_____ - _____

_____ - _____

_____ - _____

_____ - _____

_____ - _____

_____ - _____

Friends and Others (situations that I am made aware of)

Name   Specific Prayer Need

_____ - _____

_____ - _____

_____ - _____

_____ - _____

_____ - _____

Answers to Prayers & Praises

_____

_____

_____

_____

Bible Reading

Today's Date _____

Scripture God led me to read today...

_____

_____

Journaling Notes...

_____

_____

_____

_____

_____

_____

_____

_____

_____

_____

_____

_____

_____

_____

_____

_____

_____

_____

_____

_____

_____

_____

_____

_____

_____

_____

_____

_____

_____

Bible Reading

Today's Date _____

Scripture God led me to read today...

_____

_____

Journaling Notes...

_____

_____

_____

_____

_____

_____

_____

_____

_____

_____

_____

_____

_____

_____

_____

_____

_____

_____

_____

_____

_____

_____

_____

_____

_____

Bible Reading

Today's Date _____

Scripture God led me to read today...

_____

_____

Journaling Notes...

_____

_____

_____

_____

_____

_____

_____

_____

_____

_____

_____

_____

_____

_____

_____

_____

_____

_____

_____

_____

_____

_____

_____

_____

_____

_____

_____

_____

Bible Reading   Today's Date _____

Scripture God led me to read today...

_____

_____

Journaling Notes...

_____

_____

_____

_____

_____

_____

_____

_____

_____

_____

_____

_____

_____

_____

_____

_____

_____

_____

_____

_____

_____

_____

_____

_____

Bible Reading

Today's Date _____

Scripture God led me to read today...

_____
_____

Journaling Notes...

_____
_____
_____
_____
_____
_____
_____
_____
_____
_____
_____
_____
_____
_____
_____
_____
_____
_____
_____
_____
_____
_____
_____
_____
_____
_____
_____
_____

Scripture God led me to read today...

Prayer

Praise: Father, great are Your works! They are pondered by all who delight in them. Glorious and majestic are Your deeds, and Your righteousness endures forever. You have caused Your wonders to be remembered; You, Lord, are gracious and compassionate. (Psalm 111:2-4) The works of Your hands are faithful and just; all Your precepts are trustworthy. They are steadfast for ever and ever, done in faithfulness and uprightness. (Psalm 111:7-8)

Prayer List

Family — flip to the back section for strategic prayers

Name		Specific Prayer Need
_____	-	_____
_____	-	_____
_____	-	_____
_____	-	_____
_____	-	_____
_____	-	_____

Friends and Others (situations that I am made aware of)

Name		Specific Prayer Need
_____	-	_____
_____	-	_____
_____	-	_____
_____	-	_____
_____	-	_____

Answers to Prayers & Praises

_____

_____

_____

_____

Bible Reading

Today's Date _____

Scripture God led me to read today...

_____

_____

Journaling Notes...

_____

_____

_____

_____

_____

_____

_____

_____

_____

_____

_____

_____

_____

_____

_____

_____

_____

_____

_____

_____

_____

_____

_____

_____

_____

_____

Bible Reading

Today's Date _____

Scripture God led me to read today...

_____

_____

Journaling Notes...

_____

_____

_____

_____

_____

_____

_____

_____

_____

_____

_____

_____

_____

_____

_____

_____

_____

_____

_____

_____

_____

_____

_____

_____

_____

_____

Bible Reading

Today's Date _____

Scripture God led me to read today...

_____

_____

Journaling Notes...

_____

_____

_____

_____

_____

_____

_____

_____

_____

_____

_____

_____

_____

_____

_____

_____

_____

_____

_____

_____

_____

_____

_____

_____

_____

_____

_____

Bible Reading

Today's Date _____

Scripture God led me to read today...

_____

_____

Journaling Notes...

_____

_____

_____

_____

_____

_____

_____

_____

_____

_____

_____

_____

_____

_____

_____

_____

_____

_____

_____

_____

_____

_____

_____

_____

_____

_____

_____

_____

_____

Bible Reading

Today's Date _____

Scripture God led me to read today...

_____

_____

Journaling Notes...

_____

_____

_____

_____

_____

_____

_____

_____

_____

_____

_____

_____

_____

_____

_____

_____

_____

_____

_____

_____

_____

_____

_____

_____

_____

Prayer

Praise: Father, great are Your works! They are pondered by all who delight in them. Glorious and majestic are Your deeds, and Your righteousness endures forever. You have caused Your wonders to be remembered; You, Lord, are gracious and compassionate. (Psalm 111:2 4) The works of Your hands are faithful and just; all Your precepts are trustworthy. They are steadfast for ever and ever, done in faithfulness and uprightness. (Psalm 111:7-8)

Prayer List

Family— flip to the back section for strategic prayers

Name   Specific Prayer Need

_____ - _____

_____ - _____

_____ - _____

_____ - _____

_____ - _____

_____ - _____

Friends and Others (situations that I am made aware of)

Name   Specific Prayer Need

_____ - _____

_____ - _____

_____ - _____

_____ - _____

_____ - _____

Answers to Prayers & Praises

_____

_____

_____

_____

Bible Reading

Today's Date _____

Scripture God led me to read today...

_____
_____

Journaling Notes...

_____
_____
_____
_____
_____
_____
_____
_____
_____
_____
_____
_____
_____
_____
_____
_____
_____
_____
_____
_____
_____
_____
_____
_____
_____
_____
_____
_____
_____
_____

Scripture God led me to read today...

Bible Reading

Today's Date _____

Scripture God led me to read today...

_____

_____

Journaling Notes...

_____

_____

_____

_____

_____

_____

_____

_____

_____

_____

_____

_____

_____

_____

_____

_____

_____

_____

_____

_____

_____

_____

_____

_____

_____

_____

Bible Reading

Today's Date _____

Scripture God led me to read today...

_____

_____

Journaling Notes...

_____

_____

_____

_____

_____

_____

_____

_____

_____

_____

_____

_____

_____

_____

_____

_____

_____

_____

_____

_____

_____

_____

_____

_____

_____

Bible Reading

Today's Date _____

Scripture God led me to read today...

_____

_____

Journaling Notes...

_____

_____

_____

_____

_____

_____

_____

_____

_____

_____

_____

_____

_____

_____

_____

_____

_____

_____

_____

_____

_____

_____

_____

_____

_____

Bible Reading

Today's Date _____

Scripture God led me to read today...

_____
_____

Journaling Notes...

_____
_____
_____
_____
_____
_____
_____
_____
_____
_____
_____
_____
_____
_____
_____
_____
_____
_____
_____
_____
_____
_____
_____
_____
_____
_____
_____

Prayer

Praise: Father, great are Your works! They are pondered by all who delight in them. Glorious and majestic are Your deeds, and Your righteousness endures forever. You have caused Your wonders to be remembered; You, Lord, are gracious and compassionate. (Psalm 111:2-4) The works of Your hands are faithful and just; all Your precepts are trustworthy. They are steadfast for ever and ever, done in faithfulness and uprightness. (Psalm 111:7-8)

Prayer List

Family — flip to the back section for strategic prayers

Name   Specific Prayer Need

_____ - _____

_____ - _____

_____ - _____

_____ - _____

_____ - _____

_____ - _____

Friends and Others (situations that I am made aware of)

Name   Specific Prayer Need

_____ - _____

_____ - _____

_____ - _____

_____ - _____

_____ - _____

Answers to Prayers & Praises

_____

_____

_____

_____

Bible Reading

Today's Date _____

Scripture God led me to read today...

_____

_____

Journaling Notes...

_____

_____

_____

_____

_____

_____

_____

_____

_____

_____

_____

_____

_____

_____

_____

_____

_____

_____

_____

_____

_____

_____

_____

_____

_____

_____

_____

Bible Reading

Today's Date _____

Scripture God led me to read today...

_____

_____

Journaling Notes...

_____

_____

_____

_____

_____

_____

_____

_____

_____

_____

_____

_____

_____

_____

_____

_____

_____

_____

_____

_____

_____

_____

_____

_____

_____

_____

_____

_____

Bible Reading

Today's Date _____

Scripture God led me to read today...

_____

_____

Journaling Notes...

_____

_____

_____

_____

_____

_____

_____

_____

_____

_____

_____

_____

_____

_____

_____

_____

_____

_____

_____

_____

_____

_____

_____

_____

_____

_____

_____

Bible Reading

Today's Date _____

Scripture God led me to read today...

_____

_____

Journaling Notes...

_____

_____

_____

_____

_____

_____

_____

_____

_____

_____

_____

_____

_____

_____

_____

_____

_____

_____

_____

_____

_____

_____

_____

_____

Bible Reading

Today's Date _____

Scripture God led me to read today...

_____

_____

Journaling Notes...

_____

_____

_____

_____

_____

_____

_____

_____

_____

_____

_____

_____

_____

_____

_____

_____

_____

_____

_____

_____

_____

_____

_____

_____

_____

_____

_____

_____

Prayer   *Week of* _____

Praise: Father, great are Your works! They are pondered by all who delight in them. Glorious and majestic are Your deeds, and Your righteousness endures forever. You have caused Your wonders to be remembered; You, Lord, are gracious and compassionate. (Psalm 111:2-4) The works of Your hands are faithful and just; all Your precepts are trustworthy. They are steadfast for ever and ever, done in faithfulness and uprightness. (Psalm 111:7-8)

Prayer List

Family — flip to the back section for strategic prayers

Name   *Specific Prayer Need*

_____ - _____

_____ - _____

_____ - _____

_____ - _____

_____ - _____

_____ - _____

Friends and Others (situations that I am made aware of)

Name   *Specific Prayer Need*

_____ - _____

_____ - _____

_____ - _____

_____ - _____

_____ - _____

Answers to Prayers & Praises

_____

_____

_____

_____

Bible Reading

Today's Date _____

Scripture God led me to read today...

_____

_____

Journaling Notes...

_____

_____

_____

_____

_____

_____

_____

_____

_____

_____

_____

_____

_____

_____

_____

_____

_____

_____

_____

_____

_____

_____

_____

_____

_____

_____

_____

Bible Reading

Today's Date _____

Scripture God led me to read today...

_____

_____

Journaling Notes...

_____

_____

_____

_____

_____

_____

_____

_____

_____

_____

_____

_____

_____

_____

_____

_____

_____

_____

_____

_____

_____

_____

_____

_____

_____

_____

_____

_____

Bible Reading

Today's Date _____

Scripture God led me to read today...

_____

_____

Journaling Notes...

_____

_____

_____

_____

_____

_____

_____

_____

_____

_____

_____

_____

_____

_____

_____

_____

_____

_____

_____

_____

_____

_____

_____

_____

_____

Bible Reading

Today's Date _____

Scripture God led me to read today...

_____

_____

Journaling Notes...

_____

_____

_____

_____

_____

_____

_____

_____

_____

_____

_____

_____

_____

_____

_____

_____

_____

_____

_____

_____

_____

_____

_____

_____

_____

_____

Bible Reading

Today's Date _____

Scripture God led me to read today...

_____

_____

Journaling Notes...

_____

_____

_____

_____

_____

_____

_____

_____

_____

_____

_____

_____

_____

_____

_____

_____

_____

_____

_____

_____

_____

_____

_____

_____

_____

_____

_____

Scripture God led me to read today...

Prayer

Week of _____

Praise: Father, great are Your works! They are pondered by all who delight in them. Glorious and majestic are Your deeds, and Your righteousness endures forever. You have caused Your wonders to be remembered; You, Lord, are gracious and compassionate. (Psalm 111:2-4) The works of Your hands are faithful and just; all Your precepts are trustworthy. They are steadfast for ever and ever, done in faithfulness and uprightness. (Psalm 111:7-8)

Prayer List

Family — flip to the back section for strategic prayers

Name   Specific Prayer Need

_____ - _____

_____ - _____

_____ - _____

_____ - _____

_____ - _____

_____ - _____

Friends and Others (situations that I am made aware of)

Name   Specific Prayer Need

_____ - _____

_____ - _____

_____ - _____

_____ - _____

_____ - _____

_____ - _____

Answers to Prayers & Praises

_____

_____

_____

_____

Bible Reading

Today's Date _____

Scripture God led me to read today...

_____

_____

Journaling Notes...

_____

_____

_____

_____

_____

_____

_____

_____

_____

_____

_____

_____

_____

_____

_____

_____

_____

_____

_____

_____

_____

_____

_____

_____

_____

_____

Bible Reading

Today's Date _____

Scripture God led me to read today...

_____

_____

Journaling Notes...

_____

_____

_____

_____

_____

_____

_____

_____

_____

_____

_____

_____

_____

_____

_____

_____

_____

_____

_____

_____

_____

_____

_____

_____

_____

_____

_____

_____

Bible Reading

Today's Date _____

Scripture God led me to read today...

_____

_____

Journaling Notes...

_____

_____

_____

_____

_____

_____

_____

_____

_____

_____

_____

_____

_____

_____

_____

_____

_____

_____

_____

_____

_____

_____

_____

_____

_____

_____

Bible Reading

Today's Date _____

Scripture God led me to read today...

_____

_____

Journaling Notes...

_____

_____

_____

_____

_____

_____

_____

_____

_____

_____

_____

_____

_____

_____

_____

_____

_____

_____

_____

_____

_____

_____

_____

_____

_____

_____

Bible Reading

Today's Date _____

Scripture God led me to read today...

_____

_____

Journaling Notes...

_____

_____

_____

_____

_____

_____

_____

_____

_____

_____

_____

_____

_____

_____

_____

_____

_____

_____

_____

_____

_____

_____

_____

_____

_____

_____

_____

Prayer

Week of _____

Praise: Father, great are Your works! They are pondered by all who delight in them. Glorious and majestic are Your deeds, and Your righteousness endures forever. You have caused Your wonders to be remembered; You, Lord, are gracious and compassionate. (Psalm 111:2-4) The works of Your hands are faithful and just; all Your precepts are trustworthy. They are steadfast for ever and ever, done in faithfulness and uprightness. (Psalm 111:7-8)

Prayer List

Family — flip to the back section for strategic prayers

Name   Specific Prayer Need

_____ - _____

_____ - _____

_____ - _____

_____ - _____

_____ - _____

_____ - _____

Friends and Others (situations that I am made aware of)

Name   Specific Prayer Need

_____ - _____

_____ - _____

_____ - _____

_____ - _____

_____ - _____

Answers to Prayers & Praises

_____

_____

_____

_____

Bible Reading

Today's Date _____

Scripture God led me to read today...

_____

_____

Journaling Notes...

_____

_____

_____

_____

_____

_____

_____

_____

_____

_____

_____

_____

_____

_____

_____

_____

_____

_____

_____

_____

_____

_____

_____

_____

_____

_____

_____

Scripture God led me to read today...

Bible Reading

Today's Date _____

Scripture God led me to read today...

_____

_____

Journaling Notes...

_____

_____

_____

_____

_____

_____

_____

_____

_____

_____

_____

_____

_____

_____

_____

_____

_____

_____

_____

_____

_____

_____

_____

_____

_____

Bible Reading

Today's Date _____

Scripture God led me to read today...

_____

_____

Journaling Notes...

_____

_____

_____

_____

_____

_____

_____

_____

_____

_____

_____

_____

_____

_____

_____

_____

_____

_____

_____

_____

_____

_____

_____

_____

_____

_____

_____

Bible Reading

Today's Date _____

Scripture God led me to read today...

_____

_____

Journaling Notes...

_____

_____

_____

_____

_____

_____

_____

_____

_____

_____

_____

_____

_____

_____

_____

_____

_____

_____

_____

_____

_____

_____

_____

_____

_____

Bible Reading

Today's Date _____

Scripture God led me to read today...

_____

_____

Journaling Notes...

_____

_____

_____

_____

_____

_____

_____

_____

_____

_____

_____

_____

_____

_____

_____

_____

_____

_____

_____

_____

_____

_____

_____

_____

_____

_____

_____

Scripture God led me to read today...

Prayer

Week of _____

Praise: Father, great are Your works! They are pondered by all who delight in them. Glorious and majestic are Your deeds, and Your righteousness endures forever. You have caused Your wonders to be remembered; You, Lord, are gracious and compassionate. (Psalm 111:2-4) The works of Your hands are faithful and just; all Your precepts are trustworthy. They are steadfast for ever and ever, done in faithfulness and uprightness. (Psalm 111:7-8)

Prayer List

Family — flip to the back section for strategic prayers

Name   Specific Prayer Need

_____ - _____

_____ - _____

_____ - _____

_____ - _____

_____ - _____

_____ - _____

Friends and Others (situations that I am made aware of)

Name   Specific Prayer Need

_____ - _____

_____ - _____

_____ - _____

_____ - _____

_____ - _____

_____ - _____

Answers to Prayers & Praises

_____

_____

_____

_____

Bible Reading   *Today's Date* _____

Scripture God led me to read today...

_____
_____

Journaling Notes...

_____
_____
_____
_____
_____
_____
_____
_____
_____
_____
_____
_____
_____
_____
_____
_____
_____
_____
_____
_____
_____
_____
_____
_____
_____
_____
_____
_____

Scripture God led me to read today...

Bible Reading

Today's Date _____

Scripture God led me to read today...

_____

_____

Journaling Notes...

_____

_____

_____

_____

_____

_____

_____

_____

_____

_____

_____

_____

_____

_____

_____

_____

_____

_____

_____

_____

_____

_____

_____

_____

_____

_____

_____

_____

_____

_____

_____

Bible Reading

Today's Date _____

Scripture God led me to read today...

_____

_____

Journaling Notes...

_____

_____

_____

_____

_____

_____

_____

_____

_____

_____

_____

_____

_____

_____

_____

_____

_____

_____

_____

_____

_____

_____

_____

_____

_____

Bible Reading

Today's Date _____

Scripture God led me to read today...

_____

_____

Journaling Notes...

_____

_____

_____

_____

_____

_____

_____

_____

_____

_____

_____

_____

_____

_____

_____

_____

_____

_____

_____

_____

_____

_____

_____

_____

_____

_____

Bible Reading

Today's Date _____

Scripture God led me to read today...

_____

_____

Journaling Notes...

_____

_____

_____

_____

_____

_____

_____

_____

_____

_____

_____

_____

_____

_____

_____

_____

_____

_____

_____

_____

_____

_____

_____

_____

_____

_____

_____

_____

Prayer

Week of _____

Praise: Father, great are Your works! They are pondered by all who delight in them. Glorious and majestic are Your deeds, and Your righteousness endures forever. You have caused Your wonders to be remembered; You, Lord, are gracious and compassionate. (Psalm 111:2-4) The works of Your hands are faithful and just; all Your precepts are trustworthy. They are steadfast for ever and ever, done in faithfulness and uprightness. (Psalm 111:7-8)

Prayer List

Family— flip to the back section for strategic prayers

Name   Specific Prayer Need

_____ - _____

_____ - _____

_____ - _____

_____ - _____

_____ - _____

_____ - _____

Friends and Others (situations that I am made aware of)

Name   Specific Prayer Need

_____ - _____

_____ - _____

_____ - _____

_____ - _____

_____ - _____

Answers to Prayers & Praises

_____

_____

_____

_____

Bible Reading

Today's Date _____

Scripture God led me to read today...

_____
_____

Journaling Notes...

_____
_____
_____
_____
_____
_____
_____
_____
_____
_____
_____
_____
_____
_____
_____
_____
_____
_____
_____
_____
_____
_____
_____
_____
_____
_____
_____
_____

Scripture God led me to read today...

Bible Reading　　　　*Today's Date* _____

Scripture God led me to read today...

_____

_____

Journaling Notes...

_____

_____

_____

_____

_____

_____

_____

_____

_____

_____

_____

_____

_____

_____

_____

_____

_____

_____

_____

_____

_____

_____

_____

_____

_____

Bible Reading

Today's Date _____

Scripture God led me to read today...

_____

_____

Journaling Notes...

_____

_____

_____

_____

_____

_____

_____

_____

_____

_____

_____

_____

_____

_____

_____

_____

_____

_____

_____

_____

_____

_____

_____

_____

_____

_____

_____

Bible Reading   *Today's Date* _____

Scripture God led me to read today...

_____

_____

Journaling Notes...

_____

_____

_____

_____

_____

_____

_____

_____

_____

_____

_____

_____

_____

_____

_____

_____

_____

_____

_____

_____

_____

_____

_____

_____

_____

Bible Reading

Today's Date _____

Scripture God led me to read today...

_____

_____

Journaling Notes...

_____

_____

_____

_____

_____

_____

_____

_____

_____

_____

_____

_____

_____

_____

_____

_____

_____

_____

_____

_____

_____

_____

_____

_____

_____

_____

_____

_____

Prayer

Week of _____

Praise: Father, great are Your works! They are pondered by all who delight in them. Glorious and majestic are Your deeds, and Your righteousness endures forever. You have caused Your wonders to be remembered; You, Lord, are gracious and compassionate. (Psalm 111:2-4) The works of Your hands are faithful and just; all Your precepts are trustworthy. They are steadfast for ever and ever, done in faithfulness and uprightness. (Psalm 111:7-8)

Prayer List

Family— flip to the back section for strategic prayers

Name	Specific Prayer Need
_____	- _____
_____	- _____
_____	- _____
_____	- _____
_____	- _____
_____	- _____

Friends and Others (situations that I am made aware of)

Name	Specific Prayer Need
_____	- _____
_____	- _____
_____	- _____
_____	- _____
_____	- _____

Answers to Prayers & Praises

_____

_____

_____

_____

Bible Reading

Today's Date _____

Scripture God led me to read today...

_____

_____

Journaling Notes...

_____

_____

_____

_____

_____

_____

_____

_____

_____

_____

_____

_____

_____

_____

_____

_____

_____

_____

_____

_____

_____

_____

_____

_____

_____

_____

_____

_____

Bible Reading

Today's Date _____

Scripture God led me to read today...

_____

_____

Journaling Notes...

_____

_____

_____

_____

_____

_____

_____

_____

_____

_____

_____

_____

_____

_____

_____

_____

_____

_____

_____

_____

_____

_____

_____

_____

_____

_____

_____

Bible Reading

Today's Date _____

Scripture God led me to read today...

_____

_____

Journaling Notes...

_____

_____

_____

_____

_____

_____

_____

_____

_____

_____

_____

_____

_____

_____

_____

_____

_____

_____

_____

_____

_____

_____

_____

_____

_____

_____

Scripture God led me to read today...

Bible Reading

Today's Date _____

Scripture God led me to read today...

_____

_____

Journaling Notes...

_____

_____

_____

_____

_____

_____

_____

_____

_____

_____

_____

_____

_____

_____

_____

_____

_____

_____

_____

_____

_____

_____

_____

_____

_____

_____

_____

Bible Reading

Today's Date _____

Scripture God led me to read today...

_____

_____

Journaling Notes...

_____

_____

_____

_____

_____

_____

_____

_____

_____

_____

_____

_____

_____

_____

_____

_____

_____

_____

_____

_____

_____

_____

_____

_____

_____

_____

Prayer

Week of _____

Praise: Father, great are Your works! They are pondered by all who delight in them. Glorious and majestic are Your deeds, and Your righteousness endures forever. You have caused Your wonders to be remembered; You, Lord, are gracious and compassionate. (Psalm 111:2-4) The works of Your hands are faithful and just; all Your precepts are trustworthy. They are steadfast for ever and ever, done in faithfulness and uprightness. (Psalm 111:7-8)

Prayer List

Family — flip to the back section for strategic prayers

Name   Specific Prayer Need

_____ - _____

_____ - _____

_____ - _____

_____ - _____

_____ - _____

_____ - _____

Friends and Others (situations that I am made aware of)

Name   Specific Prayer Need

_____ - _____

_____ - _____

_____ - _____

_____ - _____

_____ - _____

Answers to Prayers & Praises

_____

_____

_____

_____

Bible Reading

Today's Date _____

Scripture God led me to read today...

_____

_____

Journaling Notes...

_____

_____

_____

_____

_____

_____

_____

_____

_____

_____

_____

_____

_____

_____

_____

_____

_____

_____

_____

_____

_____

_____

_____

_____

_____

_____

Bible Reading

Today's Date _____

Scripture God led me to read today...

_____

_____

Journaling Notes...

_____

_____

_____

_____

_____

_____

_____

_____

_____

_____

_____

_____

_____

_____

_____

_____

_____

_____

_____

_____

_____

_____

_____

_____

_____

Bible Reading

Today's Date _____

Scripture God led me to read today...

_____

_____

Journaling Notes...

_____

_____

_____

_____

_____

_____

_____

_____

_____

_____

_____

_____

_____

_____

_____

_____

_____

_____

_____

_____

_____

_____

_____

_____

_____

_____

_____

_____

Bible Reading

Today's Date _____

Scripture God led me to read today...

_____

_____

Journaling Notes...

_____

_____

_____

_____

_____

_____

_____

_____

_____

_____

_____

_____

_____

_____

_____

_____

_____

_____

_____

_____

_____

_____

_____

_____

_____

_____

Bible Reading

Today's Date _____

Scripture God led me to read today...

_____

_____

Journaling Notes...

_____

_____

_____

_____

_____

_____

_____

_____

_____

_____

_____

_____

_____

_____

_____

_____

_____

_____

_____

_____

_____

_____

_____

_____

_____

Scripture God led me to read today...

Prayer

Week of _____

Praise: Father, great are Your works! They are pondered by all who delight in them. Glorious and majestic are Your deeds, and Your righteousness endures forever. You have caused Your wonders to be remembered; You, Lord, are gracious and compassionate. (Psalm 111:2-4) The works of Your hands are faithful and just; all Your precepts are trustworthy. They are steadfast for ever and ever, done in faithfulness and uprightness. (Psalm 111:7-8)

Prayer List

Family — flip to the back section for strategic prayers

Name	Specific Prayer Need
_____ -	_____
_____ -	_____
_____ -	_____
_____ -	_____
_____ -	_____
_____ -	_____

Friends and Others (situations that I am made aware of)

Name	Specific Prayer Need
_____ -	_____
_____ -	_____
_____ -	_____
_____ -	_____
_____ -	_____

Answers to Prayers & Praises

_____

_____

_____

_____

Bible Reading

Today's Date _____

Scripture God led me to read today...

_____
_____

Journaling Notes...

_____
_____
_____
_____
_____
_____
_____
_____
_____
_____
_____
_____
_____
_____
_____
_____
_____
_____
_____
_____
_____
_____
_____
_____
_____
_____

Bible Reading

Today's Date _____

Scripture God led me to read today...

_____

_____

Journaling Notes...

_____

_____

_____

_____

_____

_____

_____

_____

_____

_____

_____

_____

_____

_____

_____

_____

_____

_____

_____

_____

_____

_____

_____

_____

_____

Bible Reading

Today's Date _____

Scripture God led me to read today...

_____

_____

Journaling Notes...

_____
_____
_____
_____
_____
_____
_____
_____
_____
_____
_____
_____
_____
_____
_____
_____
_____
_____
_____
_____
_____
_____
_____
_____
_____
_____

Bible Reading

Today's Date _____

Scripture God led me to read today...

_____

_____

Journaling Notes...

_____

_____

_____

_____

_____

_____

_____

_____

_____

_____

_____

_____

_____

_____

_____

_____

_____

_____

_____

_____

_____

_____

_____

_____

_____

_____

Bible Reading

Today's Date _____

Scripture God led me to read today...

_____

_____

Journaling Notes...

_____

_____

_____

_____

_____

_____

_____

_____

_____

_____

_____

_____

_____

_____

_____

_____

_____

_____

_____

_____

_____

_____

_____

_____

_____

_____

Prayer

Praise: Father, great are Your works! They are pondered by all who delight in them. Glorious and majestic are Your deeds, and Your righteousness endures forever. You have caused Your wonders to be remembered; You, Lord, are gracious and compassionate. (Psalm 111:2-4) The works of Your hands are faithful and just; all Your precepts are trustworthy. They are steadfast for ever and ever, done in faithfulness and uprightness. (Psalm 111:7-8)

Prayer List

Family — flip to the back section for strategic prayers

Name   Specific Prayer Need

_____ - _____

_____ - _____

_____ - _____

_____ - _____

_____ - _____

_____ - _____

Friends and Others (situations that I am made aware of)

Name   Specific Prayer Need

_____ - _____

_____ - _____

_____ - _____

_____ - _____

_____ - _____

Answers to Prayers & Praises

_____

_____

_____

_____

Bible Reading

Today's Date _____

Scripture God led me to read today...

_____

_____

Journaling Notes...

_____

_____

_____

_____

_____

_____

_____

_____

_____

_____

_____

_____

_____

_____

_____

_____

_____

_____

_____

_____

_____

_____

_____

_____

_____

_____

_____

_____

Bible Reading

Today's Date _____

Scripture God led me to read today...

_____

_____

Journaling Notes...

_____

_____

_____

_____

_____

_____

_____

_____

_____

_____

_____

_____

_____

_____

_____

_____

_____

_____

_____

_____

_____

_____

_____

_____

_____

_____

_____

_____

Bible Reading

Today's Date _____

Scripture God led me to read today...

_____

_____

Journaling Notes...

_____

_____

_____

_____

_____

_____

_____

_____

_____

_____

_____

_____

_____

_____

_____

_____

_____

_____

_____

_____

_____

_____

_____

_____

_____

_____

_____

Scripture God led me to read today...

Bible Reading

Today's Date _____

Scripture God led me to read today...

_____

_____

Journaling Notes...

_____

_____

_____

_____

_____

_____

_____

_____

_____

_____

_____

_____

_____

_____

_____

_____

_____

_____

_____

_____

_____

_____

_____

_____

_____

_____

_____

Bible Reading

Today's Date _____

Scripture God led me to read today...

_____

_____

Journaling Notes...

_____

_____

_____

_____

_____

_____

_____

_____

_____

_____

_____

_____

_____

_____

_____

_____

_____

_____

_____

_____

_____

_____

_____

_____

_____

Prayer

Praise: Father, great are Your works! They are pondered by all who delight in them. Glorious and majestic are Your deeds, and Your righteousness endures forever. You have caused Your wonders to be remembered; You, Lord, are gracious and compassionate. (Psalm 111:2-4) The works of Your hands are faithful and just; all Your precepts are trustworthy. They are steadfast for ever and ever, done in faithfulness and uprightness. (Psalm 111:7-8)

Prayer List

Family— flip to the back section for strategic prayers

Name   Specific Prayer Need

_____ - _____

_____ - _____

_____ - _____

_____ - _____

_____ - _____

_____ - _____

Friends and Others (situations that I am made aware of)

Name   Specific Prayer Need

_____ - _____

_____ - _____

_____ - _____

_____ - _____

_____ - _____

_____ - _____

Answers to Prayers & Praises

_____

_____

_____

_____

Bible Reading

Today's Date _____

Scripture God led me to read today...

_____

_____

Journaling Notes...

_____

_____

_____

_____

_____

_____

_____

_____

_____

_____

_____

_____

_____

_____

_____

_____

_____

_____

_____

_____

_____

_____

_____

_____

_____

_____

Bible Reading   Today's Date _____

Scripture God led me to read today...

_____

_____

Journaling Notes...

_____

_____

_____

_____

_____

_____

_____

_____

_____

_____

_____

_____

_____

_____

_____

_____

_____

_____

_____

_____

_____

_____

_____

Bible Reading

Today's Date _____

Scripture God led me to read today...

_____

_____

Journaling Notes...

_____

_____

_____

_____

_____

_____

_____

_____

_____

_____

_____

_____

_____

_____

_____

_____

_____

_____

_____

_____

_____

_____

_____

_____

Bible Reading

Today's Date _____

Scripture God led me to read today...

_____

_____

Journaling Notes...

_____

_____

_____

_____

_____

_____

_____

_____

_____

_____

_____

_____

_____

_____

_____

_____

_____

_____

_____

_____

_____

_____

_____

_____

_____

_____

Bible Reading

Today's Date _____

Scripture God led me to read today...

_____

_____

Journaling Notes...

_____

_____

_____

_____

_____

_____

_____

_____

_____

_____

_____

_____

_____

_____

_____

_____

_____

_____

_____

_____

_____

_____

_____

_____

_____

_____

_____

_____

_____

Prayer

Week of _____

Praise: Father, great are Your works! They are pondered by all who delight in them. Glorious and majestic are Your deeds, and Your righteousness endures forever. You have caused Your wonders to be remembered; You, Lord, are gracious and compassionate. (Psalm 111:2-4) The works of Your hands are faithful and just; all Your precepts are trustworthy. They are steadfast for ever and ever, done in faithfulness and uprightness. (Psalm 111:7-8)

Prayer List

Family — flip to the back section for strategic prayers

Name   Specific Prayer Need

_____   -   _____

_____   -   _____

_____   -   _____

_____   -   _____

_____   -   _____

_____   -   _____

Friends and Others (situations that I am made aware of)

Name   Specific Prayer Need

_____   -   _____

_____   -   _____

_____   -   _____

_____   -   _____

_____   -   _____

Answers to Prayers & Praises

_____

_____

_____

_____

Bible Reading

Today's Date _____

Scripture God led me to read today...

_____

_____

Journaling Notes...

_____

_____

_____

_____

_____

_____

_____

_____

_____

_____

_____

_____

_____

_____

_____

_____

_____

_____

_____

_____

_____

_____

_____

_____

_____

_____

_____

Bible Reading

Today's Date _____

Scripture God led me to read today...

_____

_____

Journaling Notes...

_____

_____

_____

_____

_____

_____

_____

_____

_____

_____

_____

_____

_____

_____

_____

_____

_____

_____

_____

_____

_____

_____

_____

_____

_____

_____

Bible Reading

Today's Date _____

Scripture God led me to read today...

_____

_____

Journaling Notes...

_____

_____

_____

_____

_____

_____

_____

_____

_____

_____

_____

_____

_____

_____

_____

_____

_____

_____

_____

_____

_____

_____

_____

_____

_____

_____

_____

Scripture God led me to read today...

Bible Reading

Today's Date _____

Scripture God led me to read today...

_____

_____

Journaling Notes...

_____

_____

_____

_____

_____

_____

_____

_____

_____

_____

_____

_____

_____

_____

_____

_____

_____

_____

_____

_____

_____

_____

_____

_____

_____

_____

Bible Reading

Today's Date _____

Scripture God led me to read today...

_____

_____

Journaling Notes...

_____

_____

_____

_____

_____

_____

_____

_____

_____

_____

_____

_____

_____

_____

_____

_____

_____

_____

_____

_____

_____

_____

_____

_____

_____

_____

_____

Prayer

Praise: Father, great are Your works! They are pondered by all who delight in them. Glorious and majestic are Your deeds, and Your righteousness endures forever. You have caused Your wonders to be remembered; You, Lord, are gracious and compassionate. (Psalm 111:2-4) The works of Your hands are faithful and just; all Your precepts are trustworthy. They are steadfast for ever and ever, done in faithfulness and uprightness. (Psalm 111:7-8)

Prayer List

Family — flip to the back section for strategic prayers

Name   Specific Prayer Need

_____ - _____

_____ - _____

_____ - _____

_____ - _____

_____ - _____

_____ - _____

Friends and Others (situations that I am made aware of)

Name   Specific Prayer Need

_____ - _____

_____ - _____

_____ - _____

_____ - _____

_____ - _____

Answers to Prayers & Praises

_____

_____

_____

Bible Reading

Today's Date _____

Scripture God led me to read today...

_____

_____

Journaling Notes...

_____

_____

_____

_____

_____

_____

_____

_____

_____

_____

_____

_____

_____

_____

_____

_____

_____

_____

_____

_____

_____

_____

_____

_____

_____

_____

_____

Bible Reading

Today's Date _____

Scripture God led me to read today...

_____

_____

Journaling Notes...

_____

_____

_____

_____

_____

_____

_____

_____

_____

_____

_____

_____

_____

_____

_____

_____

_____

_____

_____

_____

_____

_____

_____

_____

_____

_____

Bible Reading

Today's Date _____

Scripture God led me to read today...

_____

_____

Journaling Notes...

_____

_____

_____

_____

_____

_____

_____

_____

_____

_____

_____

_____

_____

_____

_____

_____

_____

_____

_____

_____

_____

_____

_____

_____

Bible Reading

Today's Date _____

Scripture God led me to read today...

_____

_____

Journaling Notes...

_____

_____

_____

_____

_____

_____

_____

_____

_____

_____

_____

_____

_____

_____

_____

_____

_____

_____

_____

_____

_____

_____

_____

_____

_____

Bible Reading

Today's Date _____

Scripture God led me to read today...

_____

_____

Journaling Notes...

_____

_____

_____

_____

_____

_____

_____

_____

_____

_____

_____

_____

_____

_____

_____

_____

_____

_____

_____

_____

_____

_____

_____

_____

_____

_____

_____

_____

_____

Prayer   *Week of* _____

Praise: Father, great are Your works! They are pondered by all who delight in them. Glorious and majestic are Your deeds, and Your righteousness endures forever. You have caused Your wonders to be remembered; You, Lord, are gracious and compassionate. (Psalm 111:2-4) The works of Your hands are faithful and just; all Your precepts are trustworthy. They are steadfast for ever and ever, done in faithfulness and uprightness. (Psalm 111:7-8)

Prayer List

Family — flip to the back section for strategic prayers

Name   *Specific Prayer Need*

_____ - _____

_____ - _____

_____ - _____

_____ - _____

_____ - _____

_____ - _____

Friends and Others (situations that I am made aware of)

Name   *Specific Prayer Need*

_____ - _____

_____ - _____

_____ - _____

_____ - _____

_____ - _____

Answers to Prayers & Praises

_____

_____

_____

_____

Bible Reading

Today's Date _____

Scripture God led me to read today...

_____
_____

Journaling Notes...

_____
_____
_____
_____
_____
_____
_____
_____
_____
_____
_____
_____
_____
_____
_____
_____
_____
_____
_____
_____
_____
_____
_____
_____
_____
_____
_____
_____

Scripture God led me to read today...

Bible Reading

Today's Date _____

Scripture God led me to read today...

_____

_____

Journaling Notes...

_____

_____

_____

_____

_____

_____

_____

_____

_____

_____

_____

_____

_____

_____

_____

_____

_____

_____

_____

_____

_____

_____

_____

_____

_____

_____

_____

Bible Reading

Today's Date _____

Scripture God led me to read today...

_____

_____

Journaling Notes...

_____

_____

_____

_____

_____

_____

_____

_____

_____

_____

_____

_____

_____

_____

_____

_____

_____

_____

_____

_____

_____

_____

_____

_____

_____

_____

_____

Scripture God led me to read today...

Bible Reading

Today's Date _____

Scripture God led me to read today...

_____

_____

Journaling Notes...

_____

_____

_____

_____

_____

_____

_____

_____

_____

_____

_____

_____

_____

_____

_____

_____

_____

_____

_____

_____

_____

_____

_____

_____

_____

Bible Reading

Today's Date _____

Scripture God led me to read today...

_____

_____

Journaling Notes...

_____

_____

_____

_____

_____

_____

_____

_____

_____

_____

_____

_____

_____

_____

_____

_____

_____

_____

_____

_____

_____

_____

_____

_____

_____

Prayer

Week of _____

Praise: Father, great are Your works! They are pondered by all who delight in them. Glorious and majestic are Your deeds, and Your righteousness endures forever. You have caused Your wonders to be remembered; You, Lord, are gracious and compassionate. (Psalm 111:2-4) The works of Your hands are faithful and just; all Your precepts are trustworthy. They are steadfast for ever and ever, done in faithfulness and uprightness. (Psalm 111:7-8)

Prayer List

Family — flip to the back section for strategic prayers

Name   Specific Prayer Need

_____ - _____

_____ - _____

_____ - _____

_____ - _____

_____ - _____

_____ - _____

Friends and Others (situations that I am made aware of)

Name   Specific Prayer Need

_____ - _____

_____ - _____

_____ - _____

_____ - _____

_____ - _____

_____ - _____

Answers to Prayers & Praises

_____

_____

_____

_____

Bible Reading

Today's Date _____

Scripture God led me to read today...

_____
_____

Journaling Notes...

_____
_____
_____
_____
_____
_____
_____
_____
_____
_____
_____
_____
_____
_____
_____
_____
_____
_____
_____
_____
_____
_____
_____
_____
_____
_____
_____
_____

Bible Reading

Today's Date _____

Scripture God led me to read today...

_____

_____

Journaling Notes...

_____

_____

_____

_____

_____

_____

_____

_____

_____

_____

_____

_____

_____

_____

_____

_____

_____

_____

_____

_____

_____

_____

_____

_____

_____

Bible Reading

Today's Date _____

Scripture God led me to read today...

_____

_____

Journaling Notes...

_____

_____

_____

_____

_____

_____

_____

_____

_____

_____

_____

_____

_____

_____

_____

_____

_____

_____

_____

_____

_____

_____

_____

_____

_____

_____

_____

_____

_____

Bible Reading

Today's Date _____

Scripture God led me to read today...

_____

_____

Journaling Notes...

_____

_____

_____

_____

_____

_____

_____

_____

_____

_____

_____

_____

_____

_____

_____

_____

_____

_____

_____

_____

_____

_____

_____

_____

Bible Reading

Today's Date _____

Scripture God led me to read today...

_____
_____

Journaling Notes...

_____
_____
_____
_____
_____
_____
_____
_____
_____
_____
_____
_____
_____
_____
_____
_____
_____
_____
_____
_____
_____
_____
_____
_____
_____
_____
_____
_____

Scripture God led me to read today...

Prayer

Week of _____

Praise: Father, great are Your works! They are pondered by all who delight in them. Glorious and majestic are Your deeds, and Your righteousness endures forever. You have caused Your wonders to be remembered; You, Lord, are gracious and compassionate. (Psalm 111:2-4) The works of Your hands are faithful and just; all Your precepts are trustworthy. They are steadfast for ever and ever, done in faithfulness and uprightness. (Psalm 111:7-8)

Prayer List

Family — flip to the back section for strategic prayers

Name   Specific Prayer Need

_____ - _____

_____ - _____

_____ - _____

_____ - _____

_____ - _____

_____ - _____

Friends and Others (situations that I am made aware of)

Name   Specific Prayer Need

_____ - _____

_____ - _____

_____ - _____

_____ - _____

_____ - _____

Answers to Prayers & Praises

_____

_____

_____

_____

Bible Reading

Today's Date _____

Scripture God led me to read today...

_____

_____

Journaling Notes...

_____

_____

_____

_____

_____

_____

_____

_____

_____

_____

_____

_____

_____

_____

_____

_____

_____

_____

_____

_____

_____

_____

_____

_____

_____

_____

_____

_____

_____

Scripture God led me to read today...

Bible Reading

Today's Date _____

Scripture God led me to read today...

_____

_____

Journaling Notes...

_____

_____

_____

_____

_____

_____

_____

_____

_____

_____

_____

_____

_____

_____

_____

_____

_____

_____

_____

_____

_____

_____

_____

_____

_____

Bible Reading

Today's Date _____

Scripture God led me to read today...

_____

_____

Journaling Notes...

_____

_____

_____

_____

_____

_____

_____

_____

_____

_____

_____

_____

_____

_____

_____

_____

_____

_____

_____

_____

_____

_____

_____

_____

_____

_____

_____

_____

Bible Reading

Today's Date _____

Scripture God led me to read today...

_____

_____

Journaling Notes...

_____

_____

_____

_____

_____

_____

_____

_____

_____

_____

_____

_____

_____

_____

_____

_____

_____

_____

_____

_____

_____

_____

_____

_____

_____

_____

Bible Reading

Today's Date _____

Scripture God led me to read today...

_____

_____

Journaling Notes...

_____
_____
_____
_____
_____
_____
_____
_____
_____
_____
_____
_____
_____
_____
_____
_____
_____
_____
_____
_____
_____
_____
_____
_____
_____
_____

Scripture God led me to read today...

Prayer

Week of _____

Praise: Father, great are Your works! They are pondered by all who delight in them. Glorious and majestic are Your deeds, and Your righteousness endures forever. You have caused Your wonders to be remembered; You, Lord, are gracious and compassionate. (Psalm 111:2-4) The works of Your hands are faithful and just; all Your precepts are trustworthy. They are steadfast for ever and ever, done in faithfulness and uprightness. (Psalm 111:7-8)

Prayer List

Family— flip to the back section for strategic prayers

Name   Specific Prayer Need

_____   - _____

_____   - _____

_____   - _____

_____   - _____

_____   - _____

_____   - _____

Friends and Others (situations that I am made aware of)

Name   Specific Prayer Need

_____   - _____

_____   - _____

_____   - _____

_____   - _____

_____   - _____

_____   - _____

Answers to Prayers & Praises

_____

_____

_____

_____

Bible Reading

Today's Date _____

Scripture God led me to read today...

_____
_____

Journaling Notes...

_____
_____
_____
_____
_____
_____
_____
_____
_____
_____
_____
_____
_____
_____
_____
_____
_____
_____
_____
_____
_____
_____
_____
_____
_____
_____

Scripture God led me to read today...

Bible Reading

Today's Date _____

Scripture God led me to read today...

_____

_____

Journaling Notes...

_____

_____

_____

_____

_____

_____

_____

_____

_____

_____

_____

_____

_____

_____

_____

_____

_____

_____

_____

_____

_____

_____

_____

_____

_____

_____

_____

_____

Bible Reading

Today's Date _____

Scripture God led me to read today...

_____

_____

Journaling Notes...

_____

_____

_____

_____

_____

_____

_____

_____

_____

_____

_____

_____

_____

_____

_____

_____

_____

_____

_____

_____

_____

_____

_____

_____

_____

_____

_____

Bible Reading

Today's Date _____

Scripture God led me to read today...

_____

_____

Journaling Notes...

_____

_____

_____

_____

_____

_____

_____

_____

_____

_____

_____

_____

_____

_____

_____

_____

_____

_____

_____

_____

_____

_____

_____

_____

_____

_____

_____

_____

Bible Reading

Today's Date _____

Scripture God led me to read today...

_____

_____

Journaling Notes...

_____

_____

_____

_____

_____

_____

_____

_____

_____

_____

_____

_____

_____

_____

_____

_____

_____

_____

_____

_____

_____

_____

_____

_____

_____

_____

_____

_____

Prayer

Week of _____

Praise: Father, great are Your works! They are pondered by all who delight in them. Glorious and majestic are Your deeds, and Your righteousness endures forever. You have caused Your wonders to be remembered; You, Lord, are gracious and compassionate. (Psalm 111:2-4) The works of Your hands are faithful and just; all Your precepts are trustworthy. They are steadfast for ever and ever, done in faithfulness and uprightness. (Psalm 111:7-8)

Prayer List

Family— flip to the back section for strategic prayers

Name   Specific Prayer Need

_____ - _____

_____ - _____

_____ - _____

_____ - _____

_____ - _____

_____ - _____

Friends and Others (situations that I am made aware of)

Name   Specific Prayer Need

_____ - _____

_____ - _____

_____ - _____

_____ - _____

_____ - _____

_____ - _____

Answers to Prayers & Praises

_____

_____

_____

_____

Bible Reading

Today's Date _____

Scripture God led me to read today...

_____
_____

Journaling Notes...

_____
_____
_____
_____
_____
_____
_____
_____
_____
_____
_____
_____
_____
_____
_____
_____
_____
_____
_____
_____
_____
_____
_____
_____
_____
_____
_____

Scripture God led me to read today...

Bible Reading

Today's Date _____

Scripture God led me to read today...

_____

_____

Journaling Notes...

_____

_____

_____

_____

_____

_____

_____

_____

_____

_____

_____

_____

_____

_____

_____

_____

_____

_____

_____

_____

_____

_____

_____

_____

_____

Bible Reading

Today's Date _____

Scripture God led me to read today...

_____

_____

Journaling Notes...

_____

_____

_____

_____

_____

_____

_____

_____

_____

_____

_____

_____

_____

_____

_____

_____

_____

_____

_____

_____

_____

_____

_____

_____

_____

_____

Bible Reading

Today's Date _____

Scripture God led me to read today...

_____

_____

Journaling Notes...

_____

_____

_____

_____

_____

_____

_____

_____

_____

_____

_____

_____

_____

_____

_____

_____

_____

_____

_____

_____

_____

_____

_____

_____

_____

_____

_____

Bible Reading   Today's Date _____

Scripture God led me to read today...

_____

_____

Journaling Notes...

_____

_____

_____

_____

_____

_____

_____

_____

_____

_____

_____

_____

_____

_____

_____

_____

_____

_____

_____

_____

_____

_____

_____

_____

Prayer

Week of _____

Praise: Father, great are Your works! They are pondered by all who delight in them. Glorious and majestic are Your deeds, and Your righteousness endures forever. You have caused Your wonders to be remembered; You, Lord, are gracious and compassionate. (Psalm 111:2-4) The works of Your hands are faithful and just; all Your precepts are trustworthy. They are steadfast for ever and ever, done in faithfulness and uprightness. (Psalm 111:7-8)

Prayer List

Family — flip to the back section for strategic prayers

Name   Specific Prayer Need

_____ - _____

_____ - _____

_____ - _____

_____ - _____

_____ - _____

_____ - _____

Friends and Others (situations that I am made aware of)

Name   Specific Prayer Need

_____ - _____

_____ - _____

_____ - _____

_____ - _____

_____ - _____

_____ - _____

Answers to Prayers & Praises

_____

_____

_____

_____

Bible Reading

Today's Date _____

Scripture God led me to read today...

_____

_____

Journaling Notes...

_____

_____

_____

_____

_____

_____

_____

_____

_____

_____

_____

_____

_____

_____

_____

_____

_____

_____

_____

_____

_____

_____

_____

_____

_____

_____

_____

Scripture God led me to read today...

Bible Reading

Today's Date _____

Scripture God led me to read today...

_____

_____

Journaling Notes...

_____

_____

_____

_____

_____

_____

_____

_____

_____

_____

_____

_____

_____

_____

_____

_____

_____

_____

_____

_____

_____

_____

_____

_____

_____

_____

Bible Reading

Today's Date _____

Scripture God led me to read today...

_____

_____

Journaling Notes...

_____

_____

_____

_____

_____

_____

_____

_____

_____

_____

_____

_____

_____

_____

_____

_____

_____

_____

_____

_____

_____

_____

_____

_____

_____

_____

Bible Reading

Today's Date _____

Scripture God led me to read today...

_____

_____

Journaling Notes...

_____

_____

_____

_____

_____

_____

_____

_____

_____

_____

_____

_____

_____

_____

_____

_____

_____

_____

_____

_____

_____

_____

_____

_____

_____

_____

_____

Bible Reading

Today's Date _____

Scripture God led me to read today...

_____

_____

Journaling Notes...

_____

_____

_____

_____

_____

_____

_____

_____

_____

_____

_____

_____

_____

_____

_____

_____

_____

_____

_____

_____

_____

_____

_____

_____

_____

_____

_____

_____

_____

Prayer

Week of _____

Praise: Father, great are Your works! They are pondered by all who delight in them. Glorious and majestic are Your deeds, and Your righteousness endures forever. You have caused Your wonders to be remembered; You, Lord, are gracious and compassionate. (Psalm 111:2-4) The works of Your hands are faithful and just; all Your precepts are trustworthy. They are steadfast for ever and ever, done in faithfulness and uprightness. (Psalm 111:7-8)

Prayer List

Family — flip to the back section for strategic prayers

Name		Specific Prayer Need
_____	-	_____
_____	-	_____
_____	-	_____
_____	-	_____
_____	-	_____
_____	-	_____

Friends and Others (situations that I am made aware of)

Name		Specific Prayer Need
_____	-	_____
_____	-	_____
_____	-	_____
_____	-	_____
_____	-	_____
_____	-	_____

Answers to Prayers & Praises

_____

_____

_____

_____

Bible Reading

Today's Date _____

Scripture God led me to read today...

_____

_____

Journaling Notes...

_____

_____

_____

_____

_____

_____

_____

_____

_____

_____

_____

_____

_____

_____

_____

_____

_____

_____

_____

_____

_____

_____

_____

_____

_____

_____

_____

_____

_____

_____

Bible Reading   Today's Date _____

Scripture God led me to read today...

_____

_____

Journaling Notes...

_____
_____
_____
_____
_____
_____
_____
_____
_____
_____
_____
_____
_____
_____
_____
_____
_____
_____
_____
_____
_____
_____
_____
_____
_____

Bible Reading

Today's Date _____

Scripture God led me to read today...

_____

_____

Journaling Notes...

_____

_____

_____

_____

_____

_____

_____

_____

_____

_____

_____

_____

_____

_____

_____

_____

_____

_____

_____

_____

_____

_____

_____

_____

Scripture God led me to read today...

Bible Reading

Today's Date _____

Scripture God led me to read today...

_____

_____

Journaling Notes...

_____

_____

_____

_____

_____

_____

_____

_____

_____

_____

_____

_____

_____

_____

_____

_____

_____

_____

_____

_____

_____

_____

_____

_____

_____

_____

Bible Reading

Today's Date _____

Scripture God led me to read today...

_____

_____

Journaling Notes...

_____

_____

_____

_____

_____

_____

_____

_____

_____

_____

_____

_____

_____

_____

_____

_____

_____

_____

_____

_____

_____

_____

_____

_____

_____

_____

_____

Scripture God led me to read today...

Prayer

Praise: Father, great are Your works! They are pondered by all who delight in them. Glorious and majestic are Your deeds, and Your righteousness endures forever. You have caused Your wonders to be remembered; You, Lord, are gracious and compassionate. (Psalm 111:2-4) The works of Your hands are faithful and just; all Your precepts are trustworthy. They are steadfast for ever and ever, done in faithfulness and uprightness. (Psalm 111:7-8)

Prayer List

Family — flip to the back section for strategic prayers

Name   Specific Prayer Need

_____ - _____

_____ - _____

_____ - _____

_____ - _____

_____ - _____

_____ - _____

Friends and Others (situations that I am made aware of)

Name   Specific Prayer Need

_____ - _____

_____ - _____

_____ - _____

_____ - _____

_____ - _____

Answers to Prayers & Praises

_____

_____

_____

_____

Bible Reading

Today's Date _____

Scripture God led me to read today...

_____

_____

Journaling Notes...

_____

_____

_____

_____

_____

_____

_____

_____

_____

_____

_____

_____

_____

_____

_____

_____

_____

_____

_____

_____

_____

_____

_____

_____

_____

_____

_____

Scripture God led me to read today...

Bible Reading   *Today's Date* _____

Scripture God led me to read today...

_____

_____

Journaling Notes...

_____

_____

_____

_____

_____

_____

_____

_____

_____

_____

_____

_____

_____

_____

_____

_____

_____

_____

_____

_____

_____

_____

_____

_____

_____

Bible Reading

Today's Date _____

Scripture God led me to read today...

_____
_____

Journaling Notes...

_____
_____
_____
_____
_____
_____
_____
_____
_____
_____
_____
_____
_____
_____
_____
_____
_____
_____
_____
_____
_____
_____
_____
_____
_____
_____
_____
_____

Scripture God led me to read today...

Bible Reading

Today's Date _____

Scripture God led me to read today...

_____

_____

Journaling Notes...

_____

_____

_____

_____

_____

_____

_____

_____

_____

_____

_____

_____

_____

_____

_____

_____

_____

_____

_____

_____

_____

_____

_____

_____

_____

Bible Reading

Today's Date _____

Scripture God led me to read today...

_____

_____

Journaling Notes...

_____

_____

_____

_____

_____

_____

_____

_____

_____

_____

_____

_____

_____

_____

_____

_____

_____

_____

_____

_____

_____

_____

_____

_____

_____

_____

_____

Scripture God led me to read today...

Prayer

Week of _____

Praise: Father, great are Your works! They are pondered by all who delight in them. Glorious and majestic are Your deeds, and Your righteousness endures forever. You have caused Your wonders to be remembered; You, Lord, are gracious and compassionate. (Psalm 111:2-4) The works of Your hands are faithful and just; all Your precepts are trustworthy. They are steadfast for ever and ever, done in faithfulness and uprightness. (Psalm 111:7-8)

Prayer List

Family — flip to the back section for strategic prayers

Name   Specific Prayer Need

_____ - _____

_____ - _____

_____ - _____

_____ - _____

_____ - _____

_____ - _____

Friends and Others (situations that I am made aware of)

Name   Specific Prayer Need

_____ - _____

_____ - _____

_____ - _____

_____ - _____

_____ - _____

_____ - _____

Answers to Prayers & Praises

_____

_____

_____

_____

Bible Reading

Today's Date _____

Scripture God led me to read today...

_____

_____

Journaling Notes...

_____

_____

_____

_____

_____

_____

_____

_____

_____

_____

_____

_____

_____

_____

_____

_____

_____

_____

_____

_____

_____

_____

_____

_____

_____

Bible Reading

Today's Date _____

Scripture God led me to read today...

_____

_____

Journaling Notes...

_____

_____

_____

_____

_____

_____

_____

_____

_____

_____

_____

_____

_____

_____

_____

_____

_____

_____

_____

_____

_____

_____

_____

_____

_____

_____

_____

_____

Bible Reading

Today's Date _____

Scripture God led me to read today...

_____

_____

Journaling Notes...

_____

_____

_____

_____

_____

_____

_____

_____

_____

_____

_____

_____

_____

_____

_____

_____

_____

_____

_____

_____

_____

_____

_____

_____

_____

Scripture God led me to read today...

Bible Reading

Today's Date _____

Scripture God led me to read today...

_____

_____

Journaling Notes...

_____

_____

_____

_____

_____

_____

_____

_____

_____

_____

_____

_____

_____

_____

_____

_____

_____

_____

_____

_____

_____

_____

_____

_____

Bible Reading   Today's Date _____

Scripture God led me to read today...

_____

_____

Journaling Notes...

_____

_____

_____

_____

_____

_____

_____

_____

_____

_____

_____

_____

_____

_____

_____

_____

_____

_____

_____

_____

_____

_____

_____

_____

_____

Prayer

Week of _____

Praise: Father, great are Your works! They are pondered by all who delight in them. Glorious and majestic are Your deeds, and Your righteousness endures forever. You have caused Your wonders to be remembered; You, Lord, are gracious and compassionate. (Psalm 111:2-4) The works of Your hands are faithful and just; all Your precepts are trustworthy. They are steadfast for ever and ever, done in faithfulness and uprightness. (Psalm 111:7-8)

Prayer List

Family — flip to the back section for strategic prayers

Name   Specific Prayer Need

_____ - _____

_____ - _____

_____ - _____

_____ - _____

_____ - _____

_____ - _____

Friends and Others (situations that I am made aware of)

Name   Specific Prayer Need

_____ - _____

_____ - _____

_____ - _____

_____ - _____

_____ - _____

Answers to Prayers & Praises

_____

_____

_____

_____

Bible Reading　　　　　*Today's Date* _____

Scripture God led me to read today...

_____

_____

Journaling Notes...

_____

_____

_____

_____

_____

_____

_____

_____

_____

_____

_____

_____

_____

_____

_____

_____

_____

_____

_____

_____

_____

_____

_____

_____

_____

_____

_____

_____

Scripture God led me to read today...

Bible Reading

Today's Date _____

Scripture God led me to read today...

_____

_____

Journaling Notes...

_____

_____

_____

_____

_____

_____

_____

_____

_____

_____

_____

_____

_____

_____

_____

_____

_____

_____

_____

_____

_____

_____

_____

_____

_____

_____

_____

Bible Reading

Today's Date _____

Scripture God led me to read today...

_____
_____

Journaling Notes...

_____
_____
_____
_____
_____
_____
_____
_____
_____
_____
_____
_____
_____
_____
_____
_____
_____
_____
_____
_____
_____
_____
_____
_____
_____
_____
_____
_____
_____

Scripture God led me to read today...

Bible Reading

Today's Date _____

Scripture God led me to read today...

_____

_____

Journaling Notes...

_____

_____

_____

_____

_____

_____

_____

_____

_____

_____

_____

_____

_____

_____

_____

_____

_____

_____

_____

_____

_____

_____

_____

_____

_____

_____

Bible Reading

Today's Date _____

Scripture God led me to read today...

_____
_____

Journaling Notes...

_____
_____
_____
_____
_____
_____
_____
_____
_____
_____
_____
_____
_____
_____
_____
_____
_____
_____
_____
_____
_____
_____
_____
_____
_____

Prayer

Week of _____

Praise: Father, great are Your works! They are pondered by all who delight in them. Glorious and majestic are Your deeds, and Your righteousness endures forever. You have caused Your wonders to be remembered; You, Lord, are gracious and compassionate. (Psalm 111:2-4) The works of Your hands are faithful and just; all Your precepts are trustworthy. They are steadfast for ever and ever, done in faithfulness and uprightness. (Psalm 111:7-8)

Prayer List

Family— flip to the back section for strategic prayers

Name   Specific Prayer Need

_____ - _____

_____ - _____

_____ - _____

_____ - _____

_____ - _____

_____ - _____

Friends and Others (situations that I am made aware of)

Name   Specific Prayer Need

_____ - _____

_____ - _____

_____ - _____

_____ - _____

_____ - _____

Answers to Prayers & Praises

_____

_____

_____

_____

Bible Reading

Today's Date _____

Scripture God led me to read today...

_____

_____

Journaling Notes...

_____
_____
_____
_____
_____
_____
_____
_____
_____
_____
_____
_____
_____
_____
_____
_____
_____
_____
_____
_____
_____
_____
_____
_____
_____
_____
_____
_____

Scripture God led me to read today...

Bible Reading

Today's Date _____

Scripture God led me to read today...

_____

_____

Journaling Notes...

_____

_____

_____

_____

_____

_____

_____

_____

_____

_____

_____

_____

_____

_____

_____

_____

_____

_____

_____

_____

_____

_____

_____

_____

_____

_____

_____

Bible Reading

Today's Date _____

Scripture God led me to read today...

_____

_____

Journaling Notes...

_____

_____

_____

_____

_____

_____

_____

_____

_____

_____

_____

_____

_____

_____

_____

_____

_____

_____

_____

_____

_____

_____

_____

_____

Scripture God led me to read today...

Bible Reading

Today's Date _____

Scripture God led me to read today...

_____

_____

Journaling Notes...

_____

_____

_____

_____

_____

_____

_____

_____

_____

_____

_____

_____

_____

_____

_____

_____

_____

_____

_____

_____

_____

_____

_____

_____

_____

_____

_____

Bible Reading   Today's Date _____

Scripture God led me to read today...

_____

_____

Journaling Notes...

_____

_____

_____

_____

_____

_____

_____

_____

_____

_____

_____

_____

_____

_____

_____

_____

_____

_____

_____

_____

_____

_____

_____

_____

Prayer

Week of _____

Praise: Father, great are Your works! They are pondered by all who delight in them. Glorious and majestic are Your deeds, and Your righteousness endures forever. You have caused Your wonders to be remembered; You, Lord, are gracious and compassionate. (Psalm 111:2-4) The works of Your hands are faithful and just; all Your precepts are trustworthy. They are steadfast for ever and ever, done in faithfulness and uprightness. (Psalm 111:7-8)

Prayer List

Family — flip to the back section for strategic prayers

Name   Specific Prayer Need

_____   -   _____

_____   -   _____

_____   -   _____

_____   -   _____

_____   -   _____

_____   -   _____

Friends and Others (situations that I am made aware of)

Name   Specific Prayer Need

_____   -   _____

_____   -   _____

_____   -   _____

_____   -   _____

_____   -   _____

Answers to Prayers & Praises

_____

_____

_____

_____

Bible Reading

Today's Date _____

Scripture God led me to read today...

_____

_____

Journaling Notes...

_____

_____

_____

_____

_____

_____

_____

_____

_____

_____

_____

_____

_____

_____

_____

_____

_____

_____

_____

_____

_____

_____

_____

_____

_____

Bible Reading

Today's Date _____

Scripture God led me to read today...

_____

_____

Journaling Notes...

_____
_____
_____
_____
_____
_____
_____
_____
_____
_____
_____
_____
_____
_____
_____
_____
_____
_____
_____
_____
_____
_____
_____
_____
_____
_____

Bible Reading

Today's Date _____

Scripture God led me to read today...

_____

_____

Journaling Notes...

_____

_____

_____

_____

_____

_____

_____

_____

_____

_____

_____

_____

_____

_____

_____

_____

_____

_____

_____

_____

_____

_____

_____

_____

_____

Bible Reading

Today's Date _____

Scripture God led me to read today...

_____

_____

Journaling Notes...

_____

_____

_____

_____

_____

_____

_____

_____

_____

_____

_____

_____

_____

_____

_____

_____

_____

_____

_____

_____

_____

_____

_____

_____

_____

Bible Reading   Today's Date _____

Scripture God led me to read today...

_____

_____

Journaling Notes...

_____

_____

_____

_____

_____

_____

_____

_____

_____

_____

_____

_____

_____

_____

_____

_____

_____

_____

_____

_____

_____

_____

_____

_____

_____

Scripture God led me to read today...

Prayer

Week of _____

Praise: Father, great are Your works! They are pondered by all who delight in them. Glorious and majestic are Your deeds, and Your righteousness endures forever. You have caused Your wonders to be remembered; You, Lord, are gracious and compassionate. (Psalm 111:2-4) The works of Your hands are faithful and just; all Your precepts are trustworthy. They are steadfast for ever and ever, done in faithfulness and uprightness. (Psalm 111:7-8)

Prayer List

Family— flip to the back section for strategic prayers

Name   Specific Prayer Need

_____ - _____

_____ - _____

_____ - _____

_____ - _____

_____ - _____

_____ - _____

Friends and Others (situations that I am made aware of)

Name   Specific Prayer Need

_____ - _____

_____ - _____

_____ - _____

_____ - _____

_____ - _____

Answers to Prayers & Praises

_____

_____

_____

_____

Bible Reading

Today's Date _____

Scripture God led me to read today...

_____
_____

Journaling Notes...

_____
_____
_____
_____
_____
_____
_____
_____
_____
_____
_____
_____
_____
_____
_____
_____
_____
_____
_____
_____
_____
_____
_____
_____
_____
_____

Scripture God led me to read today...

Bible Reading   Today's Date _____

Scripture God led me to read today...

_____

_____

Journaling Notes...

_____
_____
_____
_____
_____
_____
_____
_____
_____
_____
_____
_____
_____
_____
_____
_____
_____
_____
_____
_____
_____
_____
_____
_____
_____
_____

Bible Reading

Today's Date _____

Scripture God led me to read today...

_____

_____

Journaling Notes...

_____

_____

_____

_____

_____

_____

_____

_____

_____

_____

_____

_____

_____

_____

_____

_____

_____

_____

_____

_____

_____

_____

_____

_____

_____

_____

_____

_____

Bible Reading

Today's Date _____

Scripture God led me to read today...

_____

_____

Journaling Notes...

_____

_____

_____

_____

_____

_____

_____

_____

_____

_____

_____

_____

_____

_____

_____

_____

_____

_____

_____

_____

_____

_____

_____

_____

_____

Bible Reading

Today's Date _____

Scripture God led me to read today...

_____

_____

Journaling Notes...

_____

_____

_____

_____

_____

_____

_____

_____

_____

_____

_____

_____

_____

_____

_____

_____

_____

_____

_____

_____

_____

_____

_____

Scripture God led me to read today...

Prayer   *Week of* _____

Praise: Father, great are Your works! They are pondered by all who delight in them. Glorious and majestic are Your deeds, and Your righteousness endures forever. You have caused Your wonders to be
remembered; You, Lord, are gracious and compassionate. (Psalm 111:2-4) The works of Your hands are
faithful and just; all Your precepts are trustworthy. They are steadfast for ever and ever, done in faithfulness and uprightness. (Psalm 111:7-8)

Prayer List

Family — flip to the back section for strategic prayers

Name   *Specific Prayer Need*

_____ - _____

_____ - _____

_____ - _____

_____ - _____

_____ - _____

_____ - _____

Friends and Others (situations that I am made aware of)

Name   *Specific Prayer Need*

_____ - _____

_____ - _____

_____ - _____

_____ - _____

_____ - _____

Answers to Prayers & Praises

_____

_____

_____

_____

Bible Reading

Today's Date _____

Scripture God led me to read today...

_____

_____

Journaling Notes...

_____

_____

_____

_____

_____

_____

_____

_____

_____

_____

_____

_____

_____

_____

_____

_____

_____

_____

_____

_____

_____

_____

_____

_____

_____

_____

Scripture God led me to read today...

Bible Reading

Today's Date _____

Scripture God led me to read today...

_____

_____

Journaling Notes...

_____

_____

_____

_____

_____

_____

_____

_____

_____

_____

_____

_____

_____

_____

_____

_____

_____

_____

_____

_____

_____

_____

_____

_____

_____

_____

Bible Reading

Today's Date _____

Scripture God led me to read today...

_____
_____

Journaling Notes...

_____
_____
_____
_____
_____
_____
_____
_____
_____
_____
_____
_____
_____
_____
_____
_____
_____
_____
_____
_____
_____
_____
_____
_____
_____
_____
_____

Scripture God led me to read today...

Bible Reading

Today's Date _____

Scripture God led me to read today...

_____

_____

Journaling Notes...

_____

_____

_____

_____

_____

_____

_____

_____

_____

_____

_____

_____

_____

_____

_____

_____

_____

_____

_____

_____

_____

_____

_____

_____

_____

_____

Bible Reading   *Today's Date* _____

Scripture God led me to read today...

_____

_____

Journaling Notes...

_____

_____

_____

_____

_____

_____

_____

_____

_____

_____

_____

_____

_____

_____

_____

_____

_____

_____

_____

_____

_____

_____

_____

_____

_____

Scripture God led me to read today...

Prayer

Week of _____

Praise: Father, great are Your works! They are pondered by all who delight in them. Glorious and majestic are Your deeds, and Your righteousness endures forever. You have caused Your wonders to be remembered; You, Lord, are gracious and compassionate. (Psalm 111:2-4) The works of Your hands are faithful and just; all Your precepts are trustworthy. They are steadfast for ever and ever, done in faithfulness and uprightness. (Psalm 111:7-8)

Prayer List

Family — flip to the back section for strategic prayers

Name   Specific Prayer Need

_____ - _____

_____ - _____

_____ - _____

_____ - _____

_____ - _____

_____ - _____

Friends and Others (situations that I am made aware of)

Name   Specific Prayer Need

_____ - _____

_____ - _____

_____ - _____

_____ - _____

_____ - _____

_____ - _____

Answers to Prayers & Praises

_____

_____

_____

_____

Bible Reading

Today's Date _____

Scripture God led me to read today...

_____

_____

Journaling Notes...

_____

_____

_____

_____

_____

_____

_____

_____

_____

_____

_____

_____

_____

_____

_____

_____

_____

_____

_____

_____

_____

_____

_____

_____

_____

Scripture God led me to read today...

Bible Reading 　　　　*Today's Date* _____

Scripture God led me to read today...

_____

_____

Journaling Notes...

_____

_____

_____

_____

_____

_____

_____

_____

_____

_____

_____

_____

_____

_____

_____

_____

_____

_____

_____

_____

_____

_____

_____

_____

_____

_____

Bible Reading

Today's Date _____

Scripture God led me to read today...

_____

_____

Journaling Notes...

_____

_____

_____

_____

_____

_____

_____

_____

_____

_____

_____

_____

_____

_____

_____

_____

_____

_____

_____

_____

_____

_____

_____

_____

_____

_____

_____

Scripture God led me to read today...

Bible Reading   *Today's Date* _____

Scripture God led me to read today...

_____

_____

Journaling Notes...

_____

_____

_____

_____

_____

_____

_____

_____

_____

_____

_____

_____

_____

_____

_____

_____

_____

_____

_____

_____

_____

_____

_____

_____

_____

Bible Reading

Today's Date _____

Scripture God led me to read today...

_____

_____

Journaling Notes...

_____

_____

_____

_____

_____

_____

_____

_____

_____

_____

_____

_____

_____

_____

_____

_____

_____

_____

_____

_____

_____

_____

_____

_____

Scripture God led me to read today...

Prayer   *Week of* _____

Praise: Father, great are Your works! They are pondered by all who delight in them. Glorious and majestic are Your deeds, and Your righteousness endures forever. You have caused Your wonders to be remembered; You, Lord, are gracious and compassionate. (Psalm 111:2-4) The works of Your hands are faithful and just; all Your precepts are trustworthy. They are steadfast for ever and ever, done in faithfulness and uprightness. (Psalm 111:7-8)

Prayer List

Family — flip to the back section for strategic prayers

Name   *Specific Prayer Need*

_____ - _____

_____ - _____

_____ - _____

_____ - _____

_____ - _____

_____ - _____

Friends and Others (situations that I am made aware of)

Name   *Specific Prayer Need*

_____ - _____

_____ - _____

_____ - _____

_____ - _____

_____ - _____

_____ - _____

Answers to Prayers & Praises

_____

_____

_____

_____

Bible Reading

Today's Date _____

Scripture God led me to read today...

_____

_____

Journaling Notes...

_____

_____

_____

_____

_____

_____

_____

_____

_____

_____

_____

_____

_____

_____

_____

_____

_____

_____

_____

_____

_____

_____

_____

_____

_____

_____

Scripture God led me to read today...

Bible Reading

Today's Date _____

Scripture God led me to read today...

_____

_____

Journaling Notes...

_____

_____

_____

_____

_____

_____

_____

_____

_____

_____

_____

_____

_____

_____

_____

_____

_____

_____

_____

_____

_____

_____

_____

_____

_____

Bible Reading

Today's Date _____

Scripture God led me to read today...

_____

_____

Journaling Notes...

_____

_____

_____

_____

_____

_____

_____

_____

_____

_____

_____

_____

_____

_____

_____

_____

_____

_____

_____

_____

_____

_____

_____

_____

_____

_____

_____

Bible Reading

Today's Date _____

Scripture God led me to read today...

_____

_____

Journaling Notes...

_____

_____

_____

_____

_____

_____

_____

_____

_____

_____

_____

_____

_____

_____

_____

_____

_____

_____

_____

_____

_____

_____

_____

_____

_____

Bible Reading

Today's Date _____

Scripture God led me to read today...

_____

_____

Journaling Notes...

_____

_____

_____

_____

_____

_____

_____

_____

_____

_____

_____

_____

_____

_____

_____

_____

_____

_____

_____

_____

_____

_____

_____

_____

_____

_____

_____

Prayer

Week of _____

Praise: Father, great are Your works! They are pondered by all who delight in them. Glorious and majestic are Your deeds, and Your righteousness endures forever. You have caused Your wonders to be remembered; You, Lord, are gracious and compassionate. (Psalm 111:2-4) The works of Your hands are faithful and just; all Your precepts are trustworthy. They are steadfast for ever and ever, done in faithfulness and uprightness. (Psalm 111:7-8)

Prayer List

Family— flip to the back section for strategic prayers

Name   Specific Prayer Need

_____ - _____

_____ - _____

_____ - _____

_____ - _____

_____ - _____

_____ - _____

Friends and Others (situations that I am made aware of)

Name   Specific Prayer Need

_____ - _____

_____ - _____

_____ - _____

_____ - _____

_____ - _____

_____ - _____

Answers to Prayers & Praises

_____

_____

_____

_____

Bible Reading

Today's Date _____

Scripture God led me to read today...

_____

_____

Journaling Notes...

_____

_____

_____

_____

_____

_____

_____

_____

_____

_____

_____

_____

_____

_____

_____

_____

_____

_____

_____

_____

_____

_____

_____

_____

_____

_____

Bible Reading

Today's Date _____

Scripture God led me to read today...

_____

_____

Journaling Notes...

_____

_____

_____

_____

_____

_____

_____

_____

_____

_____

_____

_____

_____

_____

_____

_____

_____

_____

_____

_____

_____

_____

_____

_____

_____

_____

Bible Reading   Today's Date _____

Scripture God led me to read today...

_____

_____

Journaling Notes...

_____

_____

_____

_____

_____

_____

_____

_____

_____

_____

_____

_____

_____

_____

_____

_____

_____

_____

_____

_____

_____

_____

_____

_____

Scripture God led me to read today...

Bible Reading   *Today's Date* _____

Scripture God led me to read today...

_____

_____

Journaling Notes...

_____

_____

_____

_____

_____

_____

_____

_____

_____

_____

_____

_____

_____

_____

_____

_____

_____

_____

_____

_____

_____

_____

_____

_____

_____

Bible Reading

Today's Date _____

Scripture God led me to read today...

_____

_____

Journaling Notes...

_____

_____

_____

_____

_____

_____

_____

_____

_____

_____

_____

_____

_____

_____

_____

_____

_____

_____

_____

_____

_____

_____

_____

_____

_____

_____

Prayer

Praise: Father, great are Your works! They are pondered by all who delight in them. Glorious and majestic are Your deeds, and Your righteousness endures forever. You have caused Your wonders to be remembered; You, Lord, are gracious and compassionate. (Psalm 111:2-4) The works of Your hands are faithful and just; all Your precepts are trustworthy. They are steadfast for ever and ever, done in faithfulness and uprightness. (Psalm 111:7-8)

Prayer List

Family — flip to the back section for strategic prayers

Name   Specific Prayer Need

_____ - _____

_____ - _____

_____ - _____

_____ - _____

_____ - _____

_____ - _____

Friends and Others (situations that I am made aware of)

Name   Specific Prayer Need

_____ - _____

_____ - _____

_____ - _____

_____ - _____

_____ - _____

Answers to Prayers & Praises

_____

_____

_____

_____

Bible Reading

Today's Date _____

Scripture God led me to read today...

_____

_____

Journaling Notes...

_____

_____

_____

_____

_____

_____

_____

_____

_____

_____

_____

_____

_____

_____

_____

_____

_____

_____

_____

_____

_____

_____

_____

_____

Scripture God led me to read today...

Bible Reading

Today's Date _____

Scripture God led me to read today...

_____

_____

Journaling Notes...

_____

_____

_____

_____

_____

_____

_____

_____

_____

_____

_____

_____

_____

_____

_____

_____

_____

_____

_____

_____

_____

_____

_____

_____

_____

_____

_____

Bible Reading

Today's Date _____

Scripture God led me to read today...

_____

_____

Journaling Notes...

_____

_____

_____

_____

_____

_____

_____

_____

_____

_____

_____

_____

_____

_____

_____

_____

_____

_____

_____

_____

_____

_____

_____

_____

_____

_____

_____

Bible Reading

Today's Date _____

Scripture God led me to read today...

_____

_____

Journaling Notes...

_____

_____

_____

_____

_____

_____

_____

_____

_____

_____

_____

_____

_____

_____

_____

_____

_____

_____

_____

_____

_____

_____

_____

_____

Bible Reading

Today's Date _____

Scripture God led me to read today...

_____

_____

Journaling Notes...

_____

_____

_____

_____

_____

_____

_____

_____

_____

_____

_____

_____

_____

_____

_____

_____

_____

_____

_____

_____

_____

_____

_____

_____

_____

_____

Prayer

Week of _____

Praise: Father, great are Your works! They are pondered by all who delight in them. Glorious and majestic are Your deeds, and Your righteousness endures forever. You have caused Your wonders to be remembered; You, Lord, are gracious and compassionate. (Psalm 111:2-4) The works of Your hands are faithful and just; all Your precepts are trustworthy. They are steadfast for ever and ever, done in faithfulness and uprightness. (Psalm 111:7-8)

Prayer List

Family — flip to the back section for strategic prayers

Name	Specific Prayer Need
_____ -	_____
_____ -	_____
_____ -	_____
_____ -	_____
_____ -	_____
_____ -	_____

Friends and Others (situations that I am made aware of)

Name	Specific Prayer Need
_____ -	_____
_____ -	_____
_____ -	_____
_____ -	_____
_____ -	_____

Answers to Prayers & Praises

_____

_____

_____

_____

Bible Reading

Today's Date _____

Scripture God led me to read today...

_____
_____

Journaling Notes...

_____
_____
_____
_____
_____
_____
_____
_____
_____
_____
_____
_____
_____
_____
_____
_____
_____
_____
_____
_____
_____
_____
_____
_____
_____

Scripture God led me to read today...

Bible Reading

Today's Date _____

Scripture God led me to read today...

_____

_____

Journaling Notes...

_____

_____

_____

_____

_____

_____

_____

_____

_____

_____

_____

_____

_____

_____

_____

_____

_____

_____

_____

_____

_____

_____

Bible Reading

Today's Date _____

Scripture God led me to read today...

_____

_____

Journaling Notes...

_____

_____

_____

_____

_____

_____

_____

_____

_____

_____

_____

_____

_____

_____

_____

_____

_____

_____

_____

_____

_____

_____

_____

_____

_____

_____

_____

Scripture God led me to read today...

Bible Reading

Today's Date _____

Scripture God led me to read today...

_____

_____

Journaling Notes...

_____

_____

_____

_____

_____

_____

_____

_____

_____

_____

_____

_____

_____

_____

_____

_____

_____

_____

_____

_____

_____

_____

_____

_____

_____

_____

Bible Reading

Today's Date _____

Scripture God led me to read today...

_____

_____

Journaling Notes...

_____

_____

_____

_____

_____

_____

_____

_____

_____

_____

_____

_____

_____

_____

_____

_____

_____

_____

_____

_____

_____

_____

_____

_____

_____

_____

_____

Scripture God led me to read today...

Prayer

Week of _____

Praise: Father, great are Your works! They are pondered by all who delight in them. Glorious and majestic are Your deeds, and Your righteousness endures forever. You have caused Your wonders to be remembered; You, Lord, are gracious and compassionate. (Psalm 111:2-4) The works of Your hands are faithful and just; all Your precepts are trustworthy. They are steadfast for ever and ever, done in faithfulness and uprightness. (Psalm 111:7-8)

Prayer List

Family — flip to the back section for strategic prayers

Name   Specific Prayer Need

_____ - _____

_____ - _____

_____ - _____

_____ - _____

_____ - _____

_____ - _____

Friends and Others (situations that I am made aware of)

Name   Specific Prayer Need

_____ - _____

_____ - _____

_____ - _____

_____ - _____

_____ - _____

Answers to Prayers & Praises

_____

_____

_____

_____

Bible Reading

Today's Date _____

Scripture God led me to read today...

_____
_____

Journaling Notes...

_____
_____
_____
_____
_____
_____
_____
_____
_____
_____
_____
_____
_____
_____
_____
_____
_____
_____
_____
_____
_____
_____
_____
_____
_____
_____

Scripture God led me to read today...

Bible Reading

Today's Date _____

Scripture God led me to read today...

_____

_____

Journaling Notes...

_____

_____

_____

_____

_____

_____

_____

_____

_____

_____

_____

_____

_____

_____

_____

_____

_____

_____

_____

_____

_____

_____

_____

_____

_____

Bible Reading

Today's Date _____

Scripture God led me to read today…

_____

_____

Journaling Notes…

_____

_____

_____

_____

_____

_____

_____

_____

_____

_____

_____

_____

_____

_____

_____

_____

_____

_____

_____

_____

_____

_____

_____

_____

_____

_____

_____

Scripture God led me to read today…

Bible Reading

Today's Date _____

Scripture God led me to read today...

_____

_____

Journaling Notes...

_____

_____

_____

_____

_____

_____

_____

_____

_____

_____

_____

_____

_____

_____

_____

_____

_____

_____

_____

_____

_____

_____

_____

_____

_____

_____

Bible Reading

Today's Date _____

Scripture God led me to read today...

_____
_____

Journaling Notes...

_____
_____
_____
_____
_____
_____
_____
_____
_____
_____
_____
_____
_____
_____
_____
_____
_____
_____
_____
_____
_____
_____
_____
_____
_____

Scripture God led me to read today...

Prayer

Praise: Father, great are Your works! They are pondered by all who delight in them. Glorious and majestic are Your deeds, and Your righteousness endures forever. You have caused Your wonders to be remembered; You, Lord, are gracious and compassionate. (Psalm 111:2-4) The works of Your hands are faithful and just; all Your precepts are trustworthy. They are steadfast for ever and ever, done in faithfulness and uprightness. (Psalm 111:7-8)

Prayer List

Family — flip to the back section for strategic prayers

Name	Specific Prayer Need
_____ -	_____
_____ -	_____
_____ -	_____
_____ -	_____
_____ -	_____
_____ -	_____

Friends and Others (situations that I am made aware of)

Name	Specific Prayer Need
_____ -	_____
_____ -	_____
_____ -	_____
_____ -	_____
_____ -	_____

Answers to Prayers & Praises

_____

_____

_____

_____

Bible Reading

Today's Date _____

Scripture God led me to read today...

_____

_____

Journaling Notes...

_____

_____

_____

_____

_____

_____

_____

_____

_____

_____

_____

_____

_____

_____

_____

_____

_____

_____

_____

_____

_____

_____

_____

_____

_____

_____

_____

Bible Reading

Today's Date _____

Scripture God led me to read today...

_____

_____

Journaling Notes...

_____

_____

_____

_____

_____

_____

_____

_____

_____

_____

_____

_____

_____

_____

_____

_____

_____

_____

_____

_____

_____

_____

_____

_____

_____

_____

Bible Reading

Today's Date _____

Scripture God led me to read today...

_____

_____

Journaling Notes...

_____

_____

_____

_____

_____

_____

_____

_____

_____

_____

_____

_____

_____

_____

_____

_____

_____

_____

_____

_____

_____

_____

_____

_____

_____

Scripture God led me to read today...

Bible Reading

Today's Date _____

Scripture God led me to read today...

_____

_____

Journaling Notes...

_____

_____

_____

_____

_____

_____

_____

_____

_____

_____

_____

_____

_____

_____

_____

_____

_____

_____

_____

_____

_____

_____

_____

_____

_____

Bible Reading

Today's Date _____

Scripture God led me to read today...

_____

_____

Journaling Notes...

_____

_____

_____

_____

_____

_____

_____

_____

_____

_____

_____

_____

_____

_____

_____

_____

_____

_____

_____

_____

_____

_____

_____

Scripture God led me to read today...

Prayer

Week of _____

Praise: Father, great are Your works! They are pondered by all who delight in them. Glorious and majestic are Your deeds, and Your righteousness endures forever. You have caused Your wonders to be remembered; You, Lord, are gracious and compassionate. (Psalm 111:2-4) The works of Your hands are faithful and just; all Your precepts are trustworthy. They are steadfast for ever and ever, done in faithfulness and uprightness. (Psalm 111:7-8)

Prayer List

Family — flip to the back section for strategic prayers

Name   Specific Prayer Need

_____ - _____

_____ - _____

_____ - _____

_____ - _____

_____ - _____

_____ - _____

Friends and Others (situations that I am made aware of)

Name   Specific Prayer Need

_____ - _____

_____ - _____

_____ - _____

_____ - _____

_____ - _____

_____ - _____

Answers to Prayers & Praises

_____

_____

_____

_____

Bible Reading

Today's Date _____

Scripture God led me to read today...

_____

_____

Journaling Notes...

_____

_____

_____

_____

_____

_____

_____

_____

_____

_____

_____

_____

_____

_____

_____

_____

_____

_____

_____

_____

_____

_____

_____

_____

_____

_____

_____

_____

Bible Reading

Today's Date _____

Scripture God led me to read today...

_____

_____

Journaling Notes...

_____

_____

_____

_____

_____

_____

_____

_____

_____

_____

_____

_____

_____

_____

_____

_____

_____

_____

_____

_____

_____

_____

_____

_____

_____

_____

_____

_____

Bible Reading

Today's Date _____

Scripture God led me to read today...

_____

_____

Journaling Notes...

_____

_____

_____

_____

_____

_____

_____

_____

_____

_____

_____

_____

_____

_____

_____

_____

_____

_____

_____

_____

_____

_____

_____

_____

_____

_____

Scripture God led me to read today...

Bible Reading

Today's Date _____

Scripture God led me to read today...

_____

_____

Journaling Notes...

_____

_____

_____

_____

_____

_____

_____

_____

_____

_____

_____

_____

_____

_____

_____

_____

_____

_____

_____

_____

_____

_____

_____

_____

_____

_____

Bible Reading

Today's Date _____

Scripture God led me to read today...

_____

_____

Journaling Notes...

_____

_____

_____

_____

_____

_____

_____

_____

_____

_____

_____

_____

_____

_____

_____

_____

_____

_____

_____

_____

_____

_____

_____

_____

_____

_____

Scripture God led me to read today...

Prayer   *Week of* _____

Praise: Father, great are Your works! They are pondered by all who delight in them. Glorious and majestic are Your deeds, and Your righteousness endures forever. You have caused Your wonders to be remembered; You, Lord, are gracious and compassionate. (Psalm 111:2-4) The works of Your hands are faithful and just; all Your precepts are trustworthy. They are steadfast for ever and ever, done in faithfulness and uprightness. (Psalm 111:7-8)

Prayer List

Family — flip to the back section for strategic prayers

Name   *Specific Prayer Need*

_____ - _____

_____ - _____

_____ - _____

_____ - _____

_____ - _____

_____ - _____

Friends and Others (situations that I am made aware of)

Name   *Specific Prayer Need*

_____ - _____

_____ - _____

_____ - _____

_____ - _____

_____ - _____

_____ - _____

Answers to Prayers & Praises

_____

_____

_____

_____

Bible Reading

Today's Date _____

Scripture God led me to read today...

_____

_____

Journaling Notes...

_____

_____

_____

_____

_____

_____

_____

_____

_____

_____

_____

_____

_____

_____

_____

_____

_____

_____

_____

_____

_____

_____

_____

_____

_____

_____

Bible Reading

Today's Date _____

Scripture God led me to read today...

_____

_____

Journaling Notes...

_____

_____

_____

_____

_____

_____

_____

_____

_____

_____

_____

_____

_____

_____

_____

_____

_____

_____

_____

_____

_____

_____

_____

_____

Bible Reading

Today's Date _____

Scripture God led me to read today...

_____

_____

Journaling Notes...

_____

_____

_____

_____

_____

_____

_____

_____

_____

_____

_____

_____

_____

_____

_____

_____

_____

_____

_____

_____

_____

_____

_____

_____

_____

Scripture God led me to read today...

Bible Reading

Today's Date _____

Scripture God led me to read today...

_____

_____

Journaling Notes...

_____

_____

_____

_____

_____

_____

_____

_____

_____

_____

_____

_____

_____

_____

_____

_____

_____

_____

_____

_____

_____

_____

_____

_____

_____

Bible Reading

Today's Date _____

Scripture God led me to read today...

_____

_____

Journaling Notes...

_____

_____

_____

_____

_____

_____

_____

_____

_____

_____

_____

_____

_____

_____

_____

_____

_____

_____

_____

_____

_____

_____

_____

_____

Scripture God led me to read today...

Prayer

Week of _____

Praise: Father, great are Your works! They are pondered by all who delight in them. Glorious and majestic are Your deeds, and Your righteousness endures forever. You have caused Your wonders to be remembered; You, Lord, are gracious and compassionate. (Psalm 111:2-4) The works of Your hands are faithful and just; all Your precepts are trustworthy. They are steadfast for ever and ever, done in faithfulness and uprightness. (Psalm 111:7-8)

Prayer List

Family— flip to the back section for strategic prayers

Name   Specific Prayer Need

_____ - _____

_____ - _____

_____ - _____

_____ - _____

_____ - _____

_____ - _____

Friends and Others (situations that I am made aware of)

Name   Specific Prayer Need

_____ - _____

_____ - _____

_____ - _____

_____ - _____

_____ - _____

_____ - _____

Answers to Prayers & Praises

_____

_____

_____

_____

Bible Reading

Today's Date _____

Scripture God led me to read today...

_____

_____

Journaling Notes...

_____

_____

_____

_____

_____

_____

_____

_____

_____

_____

_____

_____

_____

_____

_____

_____

_____

_____

_____

_____

_____

_____

_____

_____

_____

_____

_____

Bible Reading

Today's Date _____

Scripture God led me to read today...

_____

_____

Journaling Notes...

_____

_____

_____

_____

_____

_____

_____

_____

_____

_____

_____

_____

_____

_____

_____

_____

_____

_____

_____

_____

_____

_____

_____

_____

Bible Reading

Today's Date _____

Scripture God led me to read today...

_____

_____

_____

Journaling Notes...

_____

_____

_____

_____

_____

_____

_____

_____

_____

_____

_____

_____

_____

_____

_____

_____

_____

_____

_____

_____

_____

_____

_____

_____

_____

Scripture God led me to read today...

Bible Reading

Today's Date _____

Scripture God led me to read today...

_____

_____

Journaling Notes...

_____

_____

_____

_____

_____

_____

_____

_____

_____

_____

_____

_____

_____

_____

_____

_____

_____

_____

_____

_____

_____

_____

_____

_____

_____

_____

_____

_____

Bible Reading

Today's Date _____

Scripture God led me to read today...

_____

_____

Journaling Notes...

_____

_____

_____

_____

_____

_____

_____

_____

_____

_____

_____

_____

_____

_____

_____

_____

_____

_____

_____

_____

_____

_____

_____

_____

_____

_____

_____

Prayer

Week of _____

Praise: Father, great are Your works! They are pondered by all who delight in them. Glorious and majestic are Your deeds, and Your righteousness endures forever. You have caused Your wonders to be remembered; You, Lord, are gracious and compassionate. (Psalm 111:2-4) The works of Your hands are faithful and just; all Your precepts are trustworthy. They are steadfast for ever and ever, done in faithfulness and uprightness. (Psalm 111:7-8)

Prayer List

Family — flip to the back section for strategic prayers

Name   Specific Prayer Need

_____ - _____

_____ - _____

_____ - _____

_____ - _____

_____ - _____

_____ - _____

Friends and Others (situations that I am made aware of)

Name   Specific Prayer Need

_____ - _____

_____ - _____

_____ - _____

_____ - _____

_____ - _____

Answers to Prayers & Praises

_____

_____

_____

_____

Bible Reading

Today's Date _____

Scripture God led me to read today...

_____

_____

Journaling Notes...

_____

_____

_____

_____

_____

_____

_____

_____

_____

_____

_____

_____

_____

_____

_____

_____

_____

_____

_____

_____

_____

_____

_____

_____

_____

Scripture God led me to read today...

Bible Reading

Today's Date _____

Scripture God led me to read today...

_____

_____

Journaling Notes...

_____

_____

_____

_____

_____

_____

_____

_____

_____

_____

_____

_____

_____

_____

_____

_____

_____

_____

_____

_____

_____

_____

_____

_____

_____

Bible Reading

Today's Date _____

Scripture God led me to read today...

_____

_____

Journaling Notes...

_____

_____

_____

_____

_____

_____

_____

_____

_____

_____

_____

_____

_____

_____

_____

_____

_____

_____

_____

_____

_____

_____

_____

_____

_____

_____

Bible Reading

Today's Date _____

Scripture God led me to read today...

_____

_____

Journaling Notes...

_____

_____

_____

_____

_____

_____

_____

_____

_____

_____

_____

_____

_____

_____

_____

_____

_____

_____

_____

_____

_____

_____

_____

_____

_____

_____

Bible Reading   *Today's Date* _____

Scripture God led me to read today...

_____

_____

Journaling Notes...

_____
_____
_____
_____
_____
_____
_____
_____
_____
_____
_____
_____
_____
_____
_____
_____
_____
_____
_____
_____
_____
_____
_____
_____
_____
_____

Scripture God led me to read today...

Prayer   Week of _____

Praise: Father, great are Your works! They are pondered by all who delight in them. Glorious and majestic are Your deeds, and Your righteousness endures forever. You have caused Your wonders to be
remembered; You, Lord, are gracious and compassionate. (Psalm 111:2–4) The works of Your hands are
faithful and just; all Your precepts are trustworthy. They are steadfast for ever and ever, done in faithfulness and uprightness. (Psalm 111:7–8)

Prayer List

Family — flip to the back section for strategic prayers

Name   Specific Prayer Need

_____ - _____
_____ - _____
_____ - _____
_____ - _____
_____ - _____
_____ - _____

Friends and Others (situations that I am made aware of)

Name   Specific Prayer Need

_____ - _____
_____ - _____
_____ - _____
_____ - _____
_____ - _____

Answers to Prayers & Praises

_____
_____
_____
_____

Bible Reading   *Today's Date* _____

   Scripture God led me to read today...

_____

_____

   Journaling Notes...

_____

_____

_____

_____

_____

_____

_____

_____

_____

_____

_____

_____

_____

_____

_____

_____

_____

_____

_____

_____

_____

_____

_____

_____

   Scripture God led me to read today...

Bible Reading

Today's Date _____

Scripture God led me to read today...

_____

_____

Journaling Notes...

_____

_____

_____

_____

_____

_____

_____

_____

_____

_____

_____

_____

_____

_____

_____

_____

_____

_____

_____

_____

_____

_____

_____

_____

_____

_____

Bible Reading

Today's Date _____

Scripture God led me to read today...

_____
_____

Journaling Notes...

_____
_____
_____
_____
_____
_____
_____
_____
_____
_____
_____
_____
_____
_____
_____
_____
_____
_____
_____
_____
_____
_____
_____
_____

Bible Reading

Today's Date _____

Scripture God led me to read today...

_____

_____

Journaling Notes...

_____

_____

_____

_____

_____

_____

_____

_____

_____

_____

_____

_____

_____

_____

_____

_____

_____

_____

_____

_____

_____

_____

_____

_____

_____

_____

_____

_____

Bible Reading

Today's Date _____

Scripture God led me to read today...

_____

_____

Journaling Notes...

_____

_____

_____

_____

_____

_____

_____

_____

_____

_____

_____

_____

_____

_____

_____

_____

_____

_____

_____

_____

_____

_____

_____

_____

_____

Prayer

Praise: Father, great are Your works! They are pondered by all who delight in them. Glorious and majestic are Your deeds, and Your righteousness endures forever. You have caused Your wonders to be remembered; You, Lord, are gracious and compassionate. (Psalm 111:2-4) The works of Your hands are faithful and just; all Your precepts are trustworthy. They are steadfast for ever and ever, done in faithfulness and uprightness. (Psalm 111:7-8)

Prayer List

Family — flip to the back section for strategic prayers

Name	Specific Prayer Need
_____	- _____
_____	- _____
_____	- _____
_____	- _____
_____	- _____
_____	- _____

Friends and Others (situations that I am made aware of)

Name	Specific Prayer Need
_____	- _____
_____	- _____
_____	- _____
_____	- _____
_____	- _____

Answers to Prayers & Praises

_____

_____

_____

_____

Bible Reading

Today's Date _____

Scripture God led me to read today...

_____

_____

Journaling Notes...

_____

_____

_____

_____

_____

_____

_____

_____

_____

_____

_____

_____

_____

_____

_____

_____

_____

_____

_____

_____

_____

_____

_____

_____

Scripture God led me to read today...

Bible Reading

Today's Date _____

Scripture God led me to read today...

_____

_____

Journaling Notes...

_____

_____

_____

_____

_____

_____

_____

_____

_____

_____

_____

_____

_____

_____

_____

_____

_____

_____

_____

_____

_____

_____

_____

_____

_____

Bible Reading

Today's Date _____

Scripture God led me to read today...

_____

_____

Journaling Notes...

_____

_____

_____

_____

_____

_____

_____

_____

_____

_____

_____

_____

_____

_____

_____

_____

_____

_____

_____

_____

_____

_____

_____

_____

_____

_____

_____

Bible Reading

Today's Date _____

Scripture God led me to read today...

_____
_____

Journaling Notes...

_____
_____
_____
_____
_____
_____
_____
_____
_____
_____
_____
_____
_____
_____
_____
_____
_____
_____
_____
_____
_____
_____
_____

Bible Reading

Today's Date _____

Scripture God led me to read today...

_____

_____

Journaling Notes...

_____

_____

_____

_____

_____

_____

_____

_____

_____

_____

_____

_____

_____

_____

_____

_____

_____

_____

_____

_____

_____

_____

_____

Prayer

Week of _____

Praise: Father, great are Your works! They are pondered by all who delight in them. Glorious and majestic are Your deeds, and Your righteousness endures forever. You have caused Your wonders to be remembered; You, Lord, are gracious and compassionate. (Psalm 111:2-4) The works of Your hands are faithful and just; all Your precepts are trustworthy. They are steadfast for ever and ever, done in faithfulness and uprightness. (Psalm 111:7-8)

Prayer List

Family— flip to the back section for strategic prayers

Name   Specific Prayer Need

_____ - _____

_____ - _____

_____ - _____

_____ - _____

_____ - _____

_____ - _____

Friends and Others (situations that I am made aware of)

Name   Specific Prayer Need

_____ - _____

_____ - _____

_____ - _____

_____ - _____

_____ - _____

_____

Answers to Prayers & Praises

_____

_____

_____

_____

Bible Reading

Today's Date _____

Scripture God led me to read today...

_____

_____

Journaling Notes...

_____

_____

_____

_____

_____

_____

_____

_____

_____

_____

_____

_____

_____

_____

_____

_____

_____

_____

_____

_____

_____

_____

_____

_____

Bible Reading

Today's Date _____

Scripture God led me to read today...

_____

_____

Journaling Notes...

_____

_____

_____

_____

_____

_____

_____

_____

_____

_____

_____

_____

_____

_____

_____

_____

_____

_____

_____

_____

_____

_____

_____

_____

_____

_____

_____

Bible Reading

Today's Date _____

Scripture God led me to read today...

_____

_____

Journaling Notes...

_____

_____

_____

_____

_____

_____

_____

_____

_____

_____

_____

_____

_____

_____

_____

_____

_____

_____

_____

_____

_____

_____

_____

_____

_____

_____

Scripture God led me to read today...

Bible Reading

Today's Date _____

Scripture God led me to read today...

_____

_____

Journaling Notes...

_____

_____

_____

_____

_____

_____

_____

_____

_____

_____

_____

_____

_____

_____

_____

_____

_____

_____

_____

_____

_____

_____

_____

_____

_____

_____

_____

Bible Reading

Today's Date _____

Scripture God led me to read today...

_____

_____

Journaling Notes...

_____

_____

_____

_____

_____

_____

_____

_____

_____

_____

_____

_____

_____

_____

_____

_____

_____

_____

_____

_____

_____

_____

_____

_____

_____

_____

Prayer

Week of _____

Praise: Father, great are Your works! They are pondered by all who delight in them. Glorious and majestic are Your deeds, and Your righteousness endures forever. You have caused Your wonders to be remembered; You, Lord, are gracious and compassionate. (Psalm 111:2-4) The works of Your hands are faithful and just; all Your precepts are trustworthy. They are steadfast for ever and ever, done in faithfulness and uprightness. (Psalm 111:7-8)

Prayer List

Family— flip to the back section for strategic prayers

Name   Specific Prayer Need

_____ - _____

_____ - _____

_____ - _____

_____ - _____

_____ - _____

_____ - _____

Friends and Others (situations that I am made aware of)

Name   Specific Prayer Need

_____ - _____

_____ - _____

_____ - _____

_____ - _____

_____ - _____

Answers to Prayers & Praises

_____

_____

_____

_____

Bible Reading

Today's Date _____

Scripture God led me to read today...

_____

_____

Journaling Notes...

_____

_____

_____

_____

_____

_____

_____

_____

_____

_____

_____

_____

_____

_____

_____

_____

_____

_____

_____

_____

_____

_____

_____

_____

_____

_____

Bible Reading

Today's Date _____

Scripture God led me to read today...

_____

_____

Journaling Notes...

_____

_____

_____

_____

_____

_____

_____

_____

_____

_____

_____

_____

_____

_____

_____

_____

_____

_____

_____

_____

_____

_____

_____

_____

_____

Bible Reading

Today's Date _____

Scripture God led me to read today...

_____

_____

Journaling Notes...

_____

_____

_____

_____

_____

_____

_____

_____

_____

_____

_____

_____

_____

_____

_____

_____

_____

_____

_____

_____

_____

_____

_____

_____

_____

Bible Reading

Today's Date _____

Scripture God led me to read today...

_____

_____

Journaling Notes...

_____

_____

_____

_____

_____

_____

_____

_____

_____

_____

_____

_____

_____

_____

_____

_____

_____

_____

_____

_____

_____

_____

_____

_____

Bible Reading

Today's Date _____

Scripture God led me to read today...

_____

_____

Journaling Notes...

_____
_____
_____
_____
_____
_____
_____
_____
_____
_____
_____
_____
_____
_____
_____
_____
_____
_____
_____
_____
_____
_____
_____
_____
_____

Scripture God led me to read today...

Prayer

Praise: Father, great are Your works! They are pondered by all who delight in them. Glorious and majestic are Your deeds, and Your righteousness endures forever. You have caused Your wonders to be remembered; You, Lord, are gracious and compassionate. (Psalm 111:2-4) The works of Your hands are faithful and just; all Your precepts are trustworthy. They are steadfast for ever and ever, done in faithfulness and uprightness. (Psalm 111:7-8)

Prayer List

Family — flip to the back section for strategic prayers

Name	Specific Prayer Need
_____ -	_____
_____ -	_____
_____ -	_____
_____ -	_____
_____ -	_____
_____ -	_____

Friends and Others (situations that I am made aware of)

Name	Specific Prayer Need
_____ -	_____
_____ -	_____
_____ -	_____
_____ -	_____
_____ -	_____

Answers to Prayers & Praises

_____

_____

_____

_____

Bible Reading   Today's Date _____

Scripture God led me to read today...

_____

_____

Journaling Notes...

_____

_____

_____

_____

_____

_____

_____

_____

_____

_____

_____

_____

_____

_____

_____

_____

_____

_____

_____

_____

_____

_____

_____

_____

_____

Bible Reading

Today's Date _____

Scripture God led me to read today...

_____

_____

Journaling Notes...

_____

_____

_____

_____

_____

_____

_____

_____

_____

_____

_____

_____

_____

_____

_____

_____

_____

_____

_____

_____

_____

_____

_____

_____

_____

_____

Bible Reading

Today's Date _____

Scripture God led me to read today...

_____

_____

Journaling Notes...

_____

_____

_____

_____

_____

_____

_____

_____

_____

_____

_____

_____

_____

_____

_____

_____

_____

_____

_____

_____

_____

_____

_____

_____

_____

Bible Reading

Today's Date _____

Scripture God led me to read today...

_____

_____

Journaling Notes...

_____

_____

_____

_____

_____

_____

_____

_____

_____

_____

_____

_____

_____

_____

_____

_____

_____

_____

_____

_____

_____

_____

_____

_____

_____

Bible Reading

Today's Date _____

Scripture God led me to read today...

_____

_____

Journaling Notes...

_____

_____

_____

_____

_____

_____

_____

_____

_____

_____

_____

_____

_____

_____

_____

_____

_____

_____

_____

_____

_____

_____

_____

_____

_____

Prayer

Week of _____

Praise: Father, great are Your works! They are pondered by all who delight in them. Glorious and majestic are Your deeds, and Your righteousness endures forever. You have caused Your wonders to be remembered; You, Lord, are gracious and compassionate. (Psalm 111:2-4) The works of Your hands are faithful and just; all Your precepts are trustworthy. They are steadfast for ever and ever, done in faithfulness and uprightness. (Psalm 111:7-8)

Prayer List

Family— flip to the back section for strategic prayers

Name	Specific Prayer Need
_____ -	_____
_____ -	_____
_____ -	_____
_____ -	_____
_____ -	_____
_____ -	_____

Friends and Others (situations that I am made aware of)

Name	Specific Prayer Need
_____ -	_____
_____ -	_____
_____ -	_____
_____ -	_____
_____ -	_____

Answers to Prayers & Praises

_____

_____

_____

_____

Bible Reading

Today's Date _____

Scripture God led me to read today...

_____

_____

Journaling Notes...

_____

_____

_____

_____

_____

_____

_____

_____

_____

_____

_____

_____

_____

_____

_____

_____

_____

_____

_____

_____

_____

_____

_____

_____

_____

_____

_____

Bible Reading

Today's Date _____

Scripture God led me to read today...

_____

_____

Journaling Notes...

_____
_____
_____
_____
_____
_____
_____
_____
_____
_____
_____
_____
_____
_____
_____
_____
_____
_____
_____
_____
_____
_____
_____
_____
_____
_____

Bible Reading

Today's Date _____

Scripture God led me to read today...

_____

_____

Journaling Notes...

_____

_____

_____

_____

_____

_____

_____

_____

_____

_____

_____

_____

_____

_____

_____

_____

_____

_____

_____

_____

_____

_____

_____

_____

_____

Bible Reading

Today's Date _____

Scripture God led me to read today...

_____

_____

Journaling Notes...

_____

_____

_____

_____

_____

_____

_____

_____

_____

_____

_____

_____

_____

_____

_____

_____

_____

_____

_____

_____

_____

_____

_____

_____

_____

Bible Reading   *Today's Date* _____

Scripture God led me to read today...

_____

_____

Journaling Notes...

_____

_____

_____

_____

_____

_____

_____

_____

_____

_____

_____

_____

_____

_____

_____

_____

_____

_____

_____

_____

_____

_____

_____

_____

_____

Strategic Prayers

Prayer for Myself

Dear Father, You have promised that if Your people, who are called by Your name, will humble themselves and pray and seek Your face and turn from their wicked ways, then will You hear from heaven and will forgive their sin and will heal their land. (2 Chronicles 7:14) Please help me to understand that corporate revival begins with personal, individual revival. Help me to humble myself and pray and seek Your face and turn from my own wicked ways. Thank You for hearing me from heaven and forgiving my sin and bringing healing to my heart.

PRAISE

Father, great are Your works! They are pondered by all who delight in them. Glorious and majestic are Your deeds, and Your righteousness endures forever. You have caused Your wonders to be remembered; You, Lord, are gracious and compassionate. (Psalm 111:2–4) The works of Your hands are faithful and just; all Your precepts are trustworthy. They are steadfast for ever and ever, done in faithfulness and uprightness. (Psalm 111:7–8)

CONFESSION

Dear God, I ask the Holy Spirit to rise up within me to show me anything not right; convict me.
Help me confess my sins to You now. Please help me face anything in my life that would quench Your spirit. (Take some time to confess any sins the Holy Spirit brings to your mind.)
God, I want to live victoriously. Help me to confess sin daily so nothing will hinder You. Please help me to avoid anything that would quench Your Spirit. "Create in me a clean heart, O God, and renew a right spirit within me." (Psalm 51:10)
Jesus, according to Your Word, whoever has Your commands and obeys them, he is the one who loves You. He who loves You will be loved by Your Father, and You too will love him and show Yourself to him. (John 14:21) O, God, please help me to live obediently and have the joy of seeing You revealed in all sorts of marvelous ways. Jesus, You said that "If anyone loves me, he will keep my word, and my Father will love him, and we will come to him and make our home with him." Please help me to keep Your word. I want you to make a home with me. (John 14:23)
Please help me to be an imitator of You, God, as Your beloved child. Help me to walk in love as You, Christ, loved us and gave Yourself up for us, a fragrant offering and sacrifice to God. (Ephesians 5:1)
Please help me to remember to love my neighbor as myself. (Matthew 22:39)

LOVE GOD

Lord, please give me a heart to love You and a desire to know You more than anything in life. Help me to love You with all my heart and with all my soul and with all my mind. (Matthew 22:37)
I want to be known as a child of Yours. Please help me to love You and obey Your commandments.(1 Jhn 5:2)
Sovereign Lord, Your hand has made heaven and earth, and through You they came into being. Your Word says, "This is the one I esteem: he who is humble and contrite in spirit, and trembles at my word." (Isaiah 66:2) Father, I can hardly imagine being someone You esteem, but I sincerely want to be! Make me that kind of person through the power of Your Holy Spirit.

FIX EYES ON GOD

Father, I desire to fix my eyes on Jesus, the author and perfecter of my faith, who for the joy set before Him endured the cross, scorning its shame, and sat down at the right hand of the throne of God. (Hebrews 12:2) Father, I don't want to be like the ancient Israelites who were not able to enter the Promised Land "rest" because of their unbelief. (Hebrews 3:19) Help me to believe You and follow You to the place of Your promised land in my own life.

READ BIBLE/PRAY

Just as David encouraged himself in the Lord His God, please help me to do so as well.
God, I ask you to satisfy all my longings and fill all my hollow places with Your lavish, unfailing love. Please free

me from craving the approval of others and wanting them to fill my "cup." I am asking for You to fill me up fully. Please help me to continue to fan the flame of Your love by reading Scripture, listening to edifying music, and praying often.

Father, according to Your Word, in his pride the wicked does not seek You; in all his thoughts there is no room for You. (Psalm 10:4) Please help me to always make room in my thoughts for You, God. Don't allow me to continue on in pride that stops me from seeking You.

(You may want to take a moment to pray through Psalm 104.)

Dear God, please feed my soul with Your Presence.

AGAINST EVIL ONE

My all-powerful God, enable me to stand firm, with the belt of truth buckled around my waist and with the breastplate of righteousness in place. (Ephesians 6:14) Help me to understand that without the girding of truth, I am defenseless against the devil. Truth is my main defense against the father of lies.

God, please lead me not into temptation, but deliver me from the evil one. (Matthew 6:13, NKJV)

Lord, without You I would be foolish, disobedient, deceived, and enslaved by all kinds of passions and pleasures. I would live in malice and envy, being hated and hating others. (Titus 3:3) I don't want that kind of life, God! I want to live life in the power and fullness of Your Spirit.

God, please speak truth into my heart as I confess my personal weaknesses and fears to You.

(Take some time to confess any weaknesses and fears you may have and ask God to help you overcome them.)

LIVE BY FAITH

Lord God, You have said that Your righteous one will live by faith and if he shrinks back You will not be pleased with him. (Hebrews 10:38) Lord, I want to live a life that is pleasing to You. The life that pleases you is also a life that You so readily bless. (Hebrews 11:6) I don't want to miss the great adventures You mapped out for me by shrinking back from a walk of faith.

GOOD WORKS/BEAR FRUIT

"You did not choose me, but I chose you and appointed you that you should go and bear fruit and that your fruit should abide, so that whatever you ask the Father in my name, He may give it to you." (John 15:16)

"And let us consider how to stir up one another to love and good works," (Hebrews 10:24)

"No one has ever seen God; if we love one another, God abides in us and His love is perfected in us." (1 John 4:12)

DIRECT MY PATH

Dear God, please help me to acknowledge You in all things. I ask You to make straight my path. (Prov. 3:6)

Whenever I turn to the right or to the left, I pray my ears will hear your command behind me saying, "This is the way, walk in it." (Isaiah 30:21)

Show me Your ways, O Lord, teach me Your paths; guide me in Your truth and teach me, for You are God my Savior, and my hope is in You all day long. (Psalm 25:4–5)

Father, Your Word says that if Your disciples believe, they will receive whatever they ask for in prayer. (Matthew 21:22) Lord, as you mature my faith, also teach me how to pray and what to ask of You in prayer. I have so much to learn. Keep teaching me, Father.

Lord, I know that if I ask anything according to Your will that You will hear me. And if I know that you hear me in whatever I ask, I know that I have the requests that I have asked of You. (1 John 5:14-15)

In Jesus' name I pray, Amen.

Prayer for My Husband (wife prays this)

Dear God, Your Word says that two are better than one because if one falls, the other can lift him up. Thank You for <u>(husband's name)</u>. I pray that my husband and I along with You make up a threefold cord which is hard to break. (Ecclesiastes 4:9-12)

As Head of Our Home

I acknowledge that _____ is the head of our family just as You, Jesus, are the head of the church. Please help me to submit to him in everything, as you tell me to do. I pray that You would help my husband love me as You love the church and not be harsh with me. (Ephesians 5:23-25, Colossians 3:19)

Father, help my husband to trust in You with all his heart, not depending on his own understanding, but acknowledging You in all his ways, so he knows what direction our family should take. (Proverbs 3:5-6)

His Commitment to the Lord and to His Marriage

I pray that _____ will love You with all his heart, soul, mind and strength. (Mark 12:30) I pray that he will be so committed to You, Lord, that his commitment to me will not waiver, no matter what storms come.

I pray against the spirit of divorce. (Matthew 18:18) May no thoughts of divorce or infidelity enter into my husband's heart now or in the future. Help him to take captive any thoughts that would hinder our marriage from being one that glorifies You. (2 Corinthians 10:5)

Lord, please help my husband to live with me in an understanding way so that his prayers will not be hindered in any way. (1 Peter 3:7)

Against Temptation

Lord, please lead _____ not into temptation but deliver him from the evil one. (Matthew 6:13, NKJV)

May he abhor what is evil and cling to what is good. (Romans 12:9)

His Mind

Father, give my husband the mind of Christ, saturate it with godly wisdom. Help him to take every thought captive that is not in obedience to Your Word, and in so doing protect him from pride and temptation. (1 Corinthians 2:16, 2 Corinthians 10:5)

Lord, I pray that Your Spirit covers over _____'s mind and emotions. Help him to clearly discern between Your voice and any other.

Where the enemy's lies have already invaded his thoughts, I push them back by inviting the power of the Holy Spirit to cleanse his mind. Lord, you have given me authority "over all the power of the enemy." (Luke 10:19) By that authority given to me in Jesus Christ, I command all lying spirits away from my husband's mind. I proclaim that God has given _____ a sound mind. I pray that today he will be transformed by the renewing of his mind. (Romans 12:2)

I pray Your peace, which surpasses all understanding, guard his heart and mind in Christ Jesus. (Philippians 4:6-7)

His Decisions and Work

Father, give _____ a discerning heart to know Your great love for him and the great plans You have for him and our family. Plans to prosper and not to harm, to give us hope and a future. (Jeremiah 29:11)

Whenever _____ turns to the right or to the left, I pray he will hear Your voice saying, "This is the way, walk in it." Draw him to Your path, always. (Isaiah 30:21)

Father, may the favor of the Lord rest on my husband. Bless and establish the work of his hands and his heart. (Psalm 90:17)

His Protection

Lord, please protect _____ and keep him safe. Give him wisdom and discretion so he can walk on his way securely and will not stumble or fall into danger. (Proverbs 3:21-23) Be his fortress, deliverer, rock, shield, horn of salvation and stronghold. Save him from his enemies. (Psalm 18:2-3) Make him to dwell in the shelter of Your wings. (Psalm 61:4) I pray that bad things not come near him. (Psalm 91:7) Help him to put on the whole Armor of God and stand against the schemes of the devil. (Ephesians 6:11) Preserve his going out and coming in from this time forth and forevermore. (Psalm 121:8)

His Fatherhood

I pray that you help _____ to be a good father. May he hunger and thirst to know You as his heavenly Father. May he desire to spend time in Your presence so he can become more like You, and better understand Your heart of compassion and unconditional love toward him. In turn, I pray he have this same heart toward our children. Help him to show mercy, judgment, and instruction the way You do.

Help him to have wisdom in training up our children in the way they should go. (Proverbs 22:6) May he never provoke them to wrath, but instead bring them up in the discipline and instruction of You, Lord. (Ephesians 6:4)

Please help _____ require and inspire our children to honor him as their father so that their lives will be long and blessed. (Exodus 20:12)

Lord, I pray my husband pass on a spiritual heritage to our children. Enable him to model a walk of submission to Your laws. May he delight in his children and long for them to grow up Your way.

His Faith

Lord, I pray that you help _____ firmly believe in You, Your Word, Your promises, Your ways, and Your power. May he long to spend time in Your presence—praying and reading Scripture.

Increase his faith in You. Give him unfailing certainty that You will do everything You've promised. (Romans 4:21)

Father, open the eyes of my husband's heart to understand Your Word, so that he won't be conformed to this world, but instead will be transformed by the renewing of his mind so that he may know Your good, acceptable and perfect will for his life and our marriage. (Romans 12:2)

Father, help _____ and I to live together in perfect unity by loving, honoring and respecting one another and serving each other for Your glory, honor and praise! (1 Thessalonians 5:13)

In Jesus' name, Amen.

Prayer for My Wife (husband prays this)

Dear God, Your Word says that he who finds a wife finds a good thing and has favor from You. (Proverbs 18:22) Thank you for my wife. Thank you that you saw fit that it was not good for a man to be alone, so you created a helper fit for him. (Genesis 2:18).

Your Word says that two are better than one because if one falls, the other can lift him up. I pray that my wife and I along with You make up a threefold cord which is hard to break. (Ecclesiastes 4:9-12)

Please help me to treat <u>(wife's name)</u> as You treat the church, with unconditional love and patience; mercy and forgiveness. (Colossians 3:19)

Her Commitment to the Lord and to Her Marriage

I pray that _____ will love You with all her heart, soul, mind and strength. (Mark 12:30) I pray that she will be so committed to You, Lord, that her commitment to me will not waiver, no matter what storms come.

I pray against the spirit of divorce. (Matthew 18:18) May no thoughts of divorce or infidelity enter into my wife's heart now or in the future. Help her to take captive any thoughts that would hinder our marriage from being one that glorifies You. (2 Corinthians 10:5)

I pray _____ and I always walk in love and forgiveness. (Matthew 18:21-22)

I pray _____ and I be "quick to hear, slow to speak, and slow to anger." (James 1:19)

I pray you would help us to use our words for building each other up; that our words may give grace to each other. I pray we let all bitterness, wrath, anger and slander be put away from us. Help us to be kind, tenderhearted and forgiving toward each other just as You, God, in Christ forgave us. (Ephesians 4:29-32)

Help us to love each other earnestly, since love covers a multitude of sins. (1 Peter 4:8)

Help me to render affection toward my wife and she to me. (1 Corinthians 7:3)

Please help _____ to have humility, gentleness, patience and to bear with one another in love, eager to maintain the unity of the Spirit in the bond of peace. (Ephesians 4:2-3)

Her Strength

Help my wife not to fear, but instead to be strong and courageous. Remind her that You are with her wherever she goes. (Joshua 1:9)

Please uphold my wife with Your righteous right hand. (Isaiah 41:10)

Her Self Worth and Joy

Please help _____ to know that You love her and know her by name. (Isaiah 43:1)

Each day, circumstances and frustrations can easily steal the joy from _____. Please keep her from letting these challenges turn her focus from You, the author of her faith. Give her the joy that Jesus had as He accomplished the Father's will on earth. May she consider each struggle as a reason to find hope in You and a see the struggle as tool, refining her to be more like You. (Hebrews 12:2–3, James 1:2–3)

May she know that the joy of the Lord is the source of her strength. (Nehemiah 8:10)

Her Motherhood

Protect her from growing tired of doing what You've called her to do each day. (Galatians 6:9)

When _____ feels tired, Lord, renew her strength. Surround her with friends who love You and will bear her burdens. Give her reason to feel refreshed by their encouragement. (Isaiah 40:31, Galatians 6:2, Philemon1:7)

Her Needs

Father, You supply all our needs according to Your riches in Christ. I'm amazed that you care about us enough to meet our daily concerns and to notice every detail of our lives. You give good gifts to Your children. Even the hairs of our heads are numbered because You take care of Your children. (Philippians 4:19, Matthew 7:11, 10:30)

I confess that I sometimes think of myself as being the one who takes care of _____. Forgive me for taking to myself what truly belongs to you. My wife's help comes from You. Your love and mercies never end. If she depends on me, I know I'll disappoint her. But You never fail, and You make her like a garden that always has enough water. You're always faithful, always enough. Help her to know that You are all she needs. (Psalm 121:2, Lamentations 3:22, Isaiah 58:11, John 14:8–9)

If she is tempted to look for comfort in anything else, may she instead realize how the power of Your Holy Spirit allows her to overflow with joy and peace. Nothing on this earth compares to the greatness of knowing You. (Romans 15:13, Philippians 3:8)

Protection for the Enemy

You, God, are a shield around us. You protect us from the enemy who seeks to destroy, and you will not let us be put to shame. Your arm is mighty, and Your words are powerful. (Psalm 3:3, 25:20, Exodus 15:9, Luke 1:51, Hebrews 1:3)

When the enemy attacks _____, let her faith in You protect her so that she may stand her ground. Bring your Word to her mind so that she may turn aside his assaults and fight the good fight. Help her to remember that You give us the victory through Christ. (Ephesians 6:10–18, 1 Timothy 6:12, 1 Corinthians 15:57)

You have conquered and disarmed the spiritual powers, and everything is in complete submission to You. Because of the cross, _____ is a new creation, and nothing can separate her from Your amazing, unfailing love. (Colossians 2:15, 1 Peter 3:22, 2 Corinthians 5:17, Romans 8:38–39)

The enemy is defeated. You have crushed his head. (Genesis 3:15)

Her Love

Father, You loved us first—so much so that You sent Your Son to take our place. How incredible it is to think that while we were sinners, Christ died for us. Nothing we do could ever compare to the riches of Your grace. (1 John 4:19, John 3:16, Romans 5:8, Ephesians 2:7)

Help _____ to grow in her love for You. May she be increasingly in awe of Your power, beauty, and grace. May she comprehend more each day about the breadth, length, height, and depth of Your love and respond with increasing love of her own. (Psalm 27:4, Ephesians 3:18) May she long to spend time in Your presence—praying and reading Scripture.

Help her to love me through all my failures while I learn to love her as Christ loves the church. May we see each other as You see us, and may we enjoy fulfilling each other's desires in our marriage. (Ephesians 5:25, 1 Corinthians 7:2–4)

Please give her a growing love for others in all that she does. Show her how to be Christ's ambassador in the world and to be a woman defined by love so that others may glorify You. Because of that love, may she share the gospel and herself with others. (2 Corinthians 5:20, Matthew 5:16, 1 Thessalonians 2:8)

In Jesus' Name, Amen.

Upchurch, John. Bible Gateway, http://www.biblestudytools.com/bible-study/explore-the-bible/4-prayers-every-husband-needs-to-pray-over-his-wife.html

Prayer for Troubled Marriage

Mark 10:6-9 says, "But from the beginning of creation, 'God made them male and female.' Therefore a man shall leave his father and mother and hold fast to his wife, and the two shall become one flesh.' So they are no longer two but one flesh. What therefore God has joined together, let not man separate."

Psalm 56:12 says, "Vows made to You are binding upon me, O God." I vowed to You, God, to love, honor, and cherish _____ until death. I love You, Lord. I desire to obey You by keeping that vow and fulfilling 1 Corinthians 7:10 which says, "Now to the married I command, yet not I but the Lord: a wife is not to depart from her husband." Please help me to fulfil this verse by giving _____ a heart toward reconciliation.

Dear God, please convict and remove anyone that is trying to separate _____ and me. Tear down the idols in _____'s life.

Psalm 57:10 says, "For Your mercy reaches unto the heavens, And Your truth unto the clouds."

Dear God, show _____ Your truth. Show _____ his sin so s/he can see Your great love, mercy and truth. Show him/her what Romans 5:8 says, that "while we were still sinners Christ died for us."

Give _____ a heart that longs for You, first. I pray _____ would love You with all his/her heart, soul, mind and strength. (Mark 12:30)

Give him/her a heart that longs for me. Give him/her a heart that longs for his/her family.

Ephesians 5:32 says, in reference to marriage: "This mystery is profound, and I am saying that it refers to Christ and the church." Dear God, I do believe that marriage should be a reflection of Christ and the church.

Nehemiah 2:17-18 says, "Then I said to them, 'You see the distress that we are in, how Jerusalem lies waste, and its gates burned with fire. Come and let us build the wall of Jerusalem, that we may no longer be a reproach.' And I told them of the hand of my God which had been good upon me, and also of the king's words that he had spoken to me. So they said, 'Let us rise up and build.' Then they set their hands to this good work." The wall around our marriage has been torn down. May we commit to rebuild it with Your help. I do not want my marriage to be a reproach to You. I want my marriage and my life to be one that brings You glory.

Nehemiah 2:20 says "So I answered then, and said to them, 'The God of heaven Himself will prosper us; therefore we His servants will arise and build, but you have no heritage or right or memorial in Jerusalem."

Dear God, I know that Satan has no right or memorial in my marriage. I ask that you remove him from it, in Jesus' name. Lord, remove anything or anyone that would hinder our marriage from being restored. Please cause _____ to come to his/her senses and escape the devil's snare. (2 Timothy 2:26) Tear down strongholds. Cause forgiveness to abound.

Where the enemy's lies have already invaded his/her thoughts, I push them back by inviting the power of the Holy Spirit to cleanse his/her mind. Lord, you have given me authority "over all the power of the enemy." (Luke 10:19) By that authority given to me in Jesus Christ, I command all lying spirits away from _____'s mind. I proclaim that God has given _____ a sound mind. I pray that today s/he will be transformed by the renewing of his/her mind. (Romans 12:2)

In Jesus' Name, Amen.

I pray that immediately there will fall from _____ eyes something like scales, and he/she will receive his/her sight at once; and will arise and be baptized—changed and free. (Acts 9:18)

Joel 2:25 says, "So I will restore to you the years that the swarming locust has eaten, the crawling locust, the consuming locust, and the chewing locust, My great army which I sent among you."

Dear God, please redeem what the locusts have eaten in my marriage and help us live for You. (Joel 2:25)

In Jesus' name, Amen.

Prayer for my Children

Dear God, I diligently seek You for my husband, children, church, and nation. I believe You are a rewarder of those who diligently seek You. I believe You for who You are. I pray all of this for Your honor and glory.

I ask that Your Presence fill our home with peace, love, and joy. (Galatians 5:22)

I bind the enemy - strife, contention, fear and anxiety, doubt, greed, sexual vises, negative spirits, pride, deception, self-indulgence, un-forgiveness, in the name of Jesus.

I pray that You lead <u>insert children's names</u> not into temptation, but deliver them from the evil one. (Matthew 6:13)

I pray that the blood of Jesus covers over _____ to reverse any curse in their lies and that the Spirit of God dwells there to bring life and wholeness.

I pray salvation for them - to be made whole and healed.

I declare, in the name of Jesus, that Your Spirit dwells in them; they will have a sound mind. They will have strength and healing in their bodies today. They will have a greater perception of You today, Jesus, than they had yesterday.

I pray against captivity and against anything that would control _____ besides You, God. (Isaiah 49:14-25)

I expect You to show up in _____'s lives.

I ask You for Christian friends, a good church, a Bible Study. I pray they come under the Word of God today and be accountable.

God, I ask favor for _____ with teachers (list specific teachers). I pray they learn.

I ask You for anointed pastors that speak life and hope and truth.

I pray that those people that You bring into their lives speak life and hope and encouragement.

I declare that _____ are mighty men and women for You.

I pray _____ grow in wisdom and stature and favor with You, God, and with man today. (Luke 2:52)

I pray that Your Spirit not depart from my mouth or my children's mouths from this time forth and forevermore. (Isaiah 59:21, ESV)

Help us to choose this day that, "We will serve the Lord." (Joshua 24:15)

I pray mercy and grace for my children.

Write Your Word on _____ hearts, ever working.

I know You have a plan for _____ and it is all for good as they seek You and draw near to You. (Jeremiah 29:11-13)

Please show _____ at an early age what Your plan is for their lives.

Only You provide the mates for _____.

I ask God that Your Spirit covers over their spirits, minds, emotions, and bodies. (Psalm 102:28)

Whenever _____ turn to the right or the left, I pray they hear You tell them the way to go. Draw them to Your path, always. (Isaiah 30:21)

May _____ be servants laying down our lives to You.

Put a song in _____'s hearts. (Psalm 40:3)

I pray _____ walk in love and forgiveness.

John 10:10, says the thief comes to steal, kill and destroy, but we know You, Jesus, are greater. You came to give life and life abundantly. I pray that abundant life for _____.

I pray _____ will have confidence and boldness.

I pray You teach my children and great shall be their peace. (Isaiah 54:13)

I pray You guard _____'s hearts. (Proverbs 4:23)

I pray _____ grow in wisdom and stature and favor with You, God, and with man today. (Luke 2:52)

I pray You bless _____ and keep them. Make Your face shine upon them. Raise Your countenance toward them and give them peace. (Numbers 6:24-26)

In Jesus' Name, Amen.

Prayer for Deliverance

Dear God,

2 Kings 6:17 says, "Then Elisha prayed, 'Lord, please open his eyes and let him see,' so the Lord opened the servant's eyes."

Please open _____ eyes so he/she can truly see.

Say to _____ in your way, "It is hard for you to kick against the goads." (Acts 9:5)

Thank you for looking at sin through the glass of compassion.

I pray mercy for _____. Grab him/her by the hand. (Genesis 19)

Much like Spurgeon prayed, I also pray "that the proud sinner may be brought upon his/her knees today."

Tell _____ he/she was purchased for a price. Don't let him/her go. Remind _____ he/she is Yours and break him/her in. Curb that stubborn will of his/hers.

It has to be You, God, that does this work in _____'s life.

Let _____ see how much you love him/her and may _____ be loyal to You.

Let _____ see You are pursuing him/her.

I pray that immediately there will fall from _____ eyes something like scales, and he/she will receive his/her sight at once; and will arise and be baptized—changed and free. (Acts 9:18)

I pray mercy for _____. I pray You remove the spirit of offense and pride.

"A deceived heart has turned him aside; and he cannot deliver his own soul, nor say, 'Is there not a lie in my right hand?'" (Isaiah 44:20)

Please send someone to tell _____ the truth.

Psalm 63:11 says, "But the mouth of those who speak lies shall be stopped." Thank you, God. I ask you to shut the mouths of anyone who is spreading lies and I stand on this promise that You will.

Acts 9:3-4 says, ..."suddenly a light shone around him from heaven. Then he fell to the ground, and heard a voice saying to him, "Saul, Saul, why are you persecuting Me?"

Have mercy on _____ and stop him/her so he/she can see who You are and say, "Lord, what do you want me to do?" (Acts 9:6)

May _____ fill his/her void with You and no substitutes.

I pray that You break _____ because of Your mercy; because Your love is better than life.

Sever the ties _____ has with anyone that is hindering his/her relationship with You. (Isaiah 2:22)

Be _____'s first love, God.

Help _____ surrender to You.

May _____ not be entertained by earthly pleasures which cannot compare to being awed in Your Presence.

In Jesus' Name, Amen.

Prayer Strategy for _____

_____

_____

_____

_____

_____

_____

_____

_____

_____

_____

_____

_____

_____

_____

_____

_____

_____

_____

_____

_____

_____

_____

_____

_____

_____

_____

_____

_____

_____

_____

Prayer Strategy for _____

Prayer Strategy for _____

4575622OR00188

Made in the USA
Middletown, DE
12 July 2017